THE CRISIS IN SOCIAL SECURITY:
Problems and Prospects

THE CRISIS IN SOCIAL SECURITY
Problems and Prospects

Michael J. Boskin, *Editor*
George F. Break
Rita Ricardo Campbell
Edward Cowan
Martin Feldstein
Milton Friedman
Douglas R. Munro
Sherwin Rosen
Donald O. Parsons
Carl V. Patton
Joseph A. Pechman
W. Kip Viscusi
Richard J. Zeckhauser

Institute for Contemporary Studies
San Francisco, California

All inquiries and book orders should be addressed to the Institute for Contemporary Studies, Suite 812, 260 California Street, San Francisco, California 94111—(415)-398-3010.

Library of Congress Catalog Card Number: 77-72542

ISBN 0-917616-16-2

TABLE OF CONTENTS

ERRATA   ERRATA

p. 177, lines 3 and 4: *For* in *read* to

p. 177, line 32: *For* lower fraction *read* higher fractio

CONTRIBUTORS

Michael J. Boskin
Associate Professor of Economics, Stanford University

George F. Break
Professor of Economics, University of California, Berkeley

Rita Ricardo Campbell
Senior Fellow, Hoover Institution on War, Revolution and Peace

Edward Cowan
Correspondent, Washington Bureau, NEW YORK TIMES

Martin Feldstein
Professor of Economics, Harvard University

Milton Friedman
Professor of Economics, University of Chicago

Douglas R. Munro
Assistant Professor of Economics, University of Alabama

Sherwin Rosen
Kenan Professor of Economics, University of Rochester. On leave, 1976-77, at the National Bureau of Economic Research, Stanford

Donald O. Parsons
Associate Professor of Economics, Ohio State University

Carl V. Patton
Director, Bureau of Economic and Regional Planning Research, University of Illinois

Joseph A. Pechman
Director of Economic Studies, The Brookings Institution

W. Kip Viscusi
Assistant Professor of Economics, Northwestern University

Richard J. Zeckhauser
Professor of Political Economy, Kennedy School of Government, Harvard University

PREFACE

For most of its history the social security system has enjoyed almost unique support from both the public and policymakers alike. Serious discussion of the program began only recently as the combination of inflation and demographic changes in the population drew attention to serious long term funding problems. But beyond problems of funding, empirical evidence has begun to reveal unintended, harmful effects on the economy as a whole.

Social security policy has always been governed by politics, and the current and long term funding crises are no exception. The new political problem is evident enough: payroll taxes have risen to the point where they exceed even the personal income tax for many low income families.

The security of retirement is a critical issue, and questions about social security's long run solvency have pushed the program onto the serious policymaking agenda for the first time since its inception.

Observing the rising concern of both policymakers and the public at large, the Institute asked Stanford economist Michael Boskin to assemble a group of leading students of social security, to define issues and set forth policy options. In developing the outline, special emphasis was put on the complex political issues involved—both in analyzing how present policy emerged and in considering solutions.

It is clear from the results of this effort that reform of our social security system is an urgent national priority. We trust that this book clarifies the nature of the problems, and especially emphasizes the importance of immediate action to solve them.

H. Monroe Browne
President
Institute for Contemporary Studies

San Francisco, California
April, 1977

INTRODUCTION

The social security system is the major source of retirement income for millions of Americans. For millions more it is the source of their greatest tax burden. Spawned in the Great Depression of the 1930s, social security has grown enormously; its taxes and benefits are, each, the second largest and most rapidly growing item on their respective sides of the federal budget. Despite social security's impressive accomplishments, it is in serious trouble today. The so-called trust funds are paying out more than they are taking in and, unless economic conditions improve, may soon exhaust their meager reserves; many state and local governments, believing that the system is a poor bargain for their employees, are opting out of it; many groups in the population claim that the system treats them unfairly; and, most important, an enormous long-term deficit lurks on the horizon.

Each of these issues—and others—has heightened public concern over the system's ability to continue to play a vital role in our income security system. The purpose of this book is to help focus public discussion on these issues and problems. This volume contains a series of essays by widely respected scholars, each paper designed to provide a framework for analyzing a major issue confronting this most important but least well understood income from security program. It is our hope that the book will help stimulate public discussion on the future of social security and, by raising important questions and analyzing alternatives, contribute to finding efficient and equitable solutions to fundamental problems.

Toward this end, Edward Cowan introduces, in Chapter I, a variety of social, economic, and political concerns that are now plaguing social security.

In Chapter II, Martin Feldstein, Milton Friedman, and Joseph Pechman present three different perspectives on social security. Feldstein highlights the tradeoffs inherent in social security, as well as the possibly enormous adverse incentives on private capital accumulation. Pechman argues that while the social security system is the most successful government program in U.S. history, it should move toward general revenue financing in order to reduce the tax burden on low- and middle-income workers. Friedman agrees with Pechman that general revenue financing is desirable, but for a very different reason: that decisions about social security funding would have to compete openly with other government programs and help slow their rapid growth. He also exposes a variety of myths surrounding the social security system.

In Chapter III, W. Kip Viscusi and Richard Zeckhauser present a brief guide to the relative importance of social security in the retirement income of the elderly. They also elaborate the sources of market failure that make a social insurance program desirable.

Douglas Munro and Donald Parsons present in Chapter IV evidence on the relative contributions of the insurance component and the intergenerational transfer component of social security. They suggest that the benefits received by retirees today are far in excess of taxes paid plus interest, although this excess—or transfer from current workers—is declining through time.

Sherwin Rosen, in Chapter V, imbeds the analysis of social security in the context of the overall economy, particularly the intrafamily pattern of capital accumulation and income transfer. He presents an appropriate framework for comparing the (implicit) rate of return on social security with that on private insurance. He also discusses the potential adverse incentives created by social security on private saving for retirement and on the labor supply of elderly workers.

In Chapter VI, George Break dissects the major features of social security taxes. He discusses why economists believe the employer's share of the payroll tax is ultimately paid by workers.

He also focuses on the important issue of the public's perception of social security taxes and the implication of this for financing the program.

Rita Campbell, Chapter VII, discusses the perceived inequities of the program and the demands of several groups in the population, particularly women, for reform of the relationship between benefits and taxes.

Carl Patton analyzes the politics of social security in Chapter VIII. After discussing the political considerations surrounding social security throughout its development, he analyzes the political costs and benefits associated with alternative reforms.

In Chapter IX, I conclude with a discussion of the dramatic changes which have occurred in the economy since the inception of social security and the implications of these changes for the social security system. Paying particular attention to three related sets of problems, inequities, adverse incentives, and long-term funding crisis, I conclude with my own general set of policy proposals.

Finally, the authors would like to thank Monroe Browne, Lawrence Chickering, and the staff of the Institute for Contemporary Studies for their encouragement and extensive editorial support in the production of this volume.

Michael J. Boskin

Stanford, California
February 1977

I

EDWARD COWAN

BACKGROUND AND HISTORY: THE CRISIS IN PUBLIC FINANCE AND SOCIAL SECURITY

Brief history. Rationale and reality. The growing deficit. Demographic changes, inflation, and double inflation adjustment. Replacement ratios. The long term deficit. Public employee withdrawals. The earnings test. Other problems of fairness. The long term prospect.

Social security, the most enduring and politically influential legacy of President Franklin D. Roosevelt's New Deal era of governance, is going through a crisis. Deficits are at hand and in prospect— small ones in the next few years, perhaps frighteningly large ones in the twenty-first century. Something must be done.

The remedy will not be trivial. It will involve large sums of money. It could also involve basic changes in the way old age, survivor, and disability benefits are calculated and financed.

1

Mandated by the Social Security Act of 1935 and liberalized by amendments in 1939 and later, the social security system has grown to be an important part of the income structure of the American economy. To 32.7 million Americans, "Social Security" means a check in the mail once a month—a total of $6.3 billion a month, $75 billion a year, of purchasing power. In 1976, benefits to retired persons averaged $223 a month; to the disabled, $244.[1]

The system, as put in place by Roosevelt and his associates, was meant to be self-supporting by means of a payroll tax. The initial levy, 2 percent of the first $3,000 of earnings to be split evenly between employer and employee, amounted to payments by each of $30 a year. That so-called "1 percent" tax rate—the popular way of viewing the levy is to look only at the sum withheld from the paycheck—prevailed until 1949. By 1977 the levy had climbed to 11.7 percent—or 5.85 percent withheld—on the first $16,500 of earnings. From $30 a year, the social security tax withheld from paychecks has climbed to $965.25. The causes of this soaring trend are several: the natural evolution of the program as the number of beneficiaries grew, greater longevity, improvements in benefits voted repeatedly by Congress, introduction of Medicare benefits for the aged, inflation, resistance in Congress to the possibility of financing social security (in part) from the general revenues of the Treasury.

RATIONALE AND REALITY

As originally presented to the public in 1935, social security was a conservative pension system that seemed to resemble private insurance. In fact, it was not an insurance system but a way of having the working-age population contribute to the support of the aged, an intergenerational system of transfer payments through the federal government. The young support the old, believing that in their turn they will be supported by the young. This has been an essential proposition of family life—and still is, for many families. With social security, the system is writ large. It is compulsory, nearly universal, and—perhaps most important—virtually immune to the risk of economic distress, a risk few families can fully insure against.

It is unthinkable that the government of the United States would be unable to meet its social security commitments, would be unable to make those 32.7 million payments on time every month. Yet as unimaginable as that may be, social security is in trouble. In 1976 the system paid out an estimated $4.3 billion more than it took in from payroll taxes and the levy paid by the self-employed.[2] The old age trust fund financed this deficit. But by the end of 1976 the fund's assets had shrunk to an estimated $34.3 billion.[3] With further deficits in prospect, some change plainly had to be made to achieve a sounder financial footing.

Changing the way social security operates almost surely means that some citizens will gain, others will lose. Changes in ongoing federal programs that affect large numbers of persons rarely are neutral. In social security, changes may give rise to a crisis of confidence. Indeed, it may be that a crisis of confidence is already developing. Members of Congress report that anxious inquiries flood their offices whenever social security financing issues and uncertainties are in the news, as they occasionally have been for several years. The elderly fear for the solvency of the system. They fear that their monthly checks will stop.

Although intended to be only a part of retirement income, social security has come to be a principal or sole source of old-age sustenance for millions of elderly persons. It is probable that no other federal issue except the personal income tax touches as many voters or is as closely watched by them. For elected politicians, whose thoughts are rarely far from the next election, that makes social security a politically dangerous issue. No wonder that Carl Vernon Patton writes in his chapter in this book that "politics will continue to be the largest single influence on policy." The social security crisis, then, is an amalgam of fiscal or actuarial problems and equity issues about taking and giving, all overlaid with acute political sensitivity.

THE GROWING DEFICIT

In the years since the presidency of Dwight D. Eisenhower, Washington has accepted budget deficits as a regular part of the American economic system. In recent years the question for economic forecasters has not been whether the federal budget would have a deficit, but how much that deficit would be.

This comparatively sophisticated approach to deficits does not carry over to social security, for which a more traditional view still prevails, a view that shuns deficits. In the beginning, as Patton recalls, President Roosevelt intended that social security payroll tax revenues cover the outlays. In the 1950s and 1960s Congress reaffirmed that principle. Deficits in several years between 1957 and 1965 were small and were financed from the old age and survivors insurance trust fund, which was functioning as a rainy-day account as it was intended to do. But although the system as a whole was paying its own way, the size of the trust fund in relation to annual disbursements was falling from a ratio of 3 to 1 in 1957 to unity in 1965.

For a program dedicated to budget surpluses, social security red ink was news.

It was with a sense of shock that the *Wall Street Journal* reported on 27 February 1975 as headline for a front-page story: "Social Security System Is on Way to Going Broke, Analysts Warn; Payments Outstrip Income; Arguments Are Growing on How to Stop Deficits."

The problem of how to finance social security benefits is at once old and recent. Frances Perkins, who was FDR's Secretary of Labor and a major advocate of a social insurance system, recalled that "Roosevelt was determined to have a bona fide self-maintaining system," but that even in 1935 the planners foresaw that "perhaps in 1980 it would be necessary for the Congress to appropriate money to make up a deficit."[4]

Despite the historical propensity of Congress to sweeten benefits by more than it raised the social security payroll tax, no general issue of social security financing arose until publication of the 1974 report by the four social security trustees, the secretaries of the Treasury, Labor and Health, Education and Welfare, and the Commissioner of Social Security. The 1974 report anticipated the first sizable actuarial imbalances. The subsequent two annual reports painted increasingly worse pictures. The problem in 1976 was presented as follows:[5]

A deficit of benefit payments in excess of outlays loomed for every calendar year from 1976 to 2050. Figure 1* shows the picture. Under an intermediate set of assumptions about economic growth, the average annual deficit for the six-year period 1976-1981 would be 0.82 percent of taxable earnings. The steady six-year drain on the old age and survivors trust fund would shrink it from $37 billion in 1975 to $17.9 billion at the end of 1981. By 1984 it would be exhausted. The least favorable assumptions showed the trust fund wiped out by 1981.

As required by law, the trustees in their 1976 report also took a long-range look at the system. Under their intermediate assumptions, they projected deficits of 1.91 percent of taxable earnings for the years 1976-2000; 6.85 percent for 2001-2025; and 15.14 percent for 2026-2050. The average for the seventy-five years was 7.96 percent.

Projections such as these do, indeed, justify newspaper headlines about "going broke." But are the projections themselves justified? The trustees place the figures in perspective as follows:

> These deficits, particularly for the period after the year 2000, should be interpreted with caution because they are based upon future benefit levels which are much higher, relative to preretirement earnings, than are currently prevailing benefit levels and which will not materialize if realistic legislation is enacted to redress the imbalance.[6]

Figure 1 shows the trustees' own "more realistic" outlook, or "modified theoretical system," which was based on an assumed change in the law that would maintain through time the ratio of average benefits to preretirement earnings and called for annual deficits for the three 25-year periods of 1.68 percent, 3.81 percent, and 7.40 percent, with an overall average of 4.28 percent.[7]

*The charts and figures shown herein are based upon assumptions and methodology explained in detail in the 1976 annual reports of the Board of Trustees of the Federal Old-Age and Survivors Insurance and Disability Insurance Trust Funds, the Hospital Insurance Trust Fund, and the Supplementary Medical Insurance Trust Fund. All figures are based upon the intermediate set of assumptions contained in those reports.

Old-Age, Survivors, and Disability
Insurance Program

FIGURE 1

Projected Expenditures under Present Law and under an Illustrative Alternative Law (with Stable Replacement Ratios); and Tax Income under Present Law; Expressed as a Percentage of Taxable Payroll

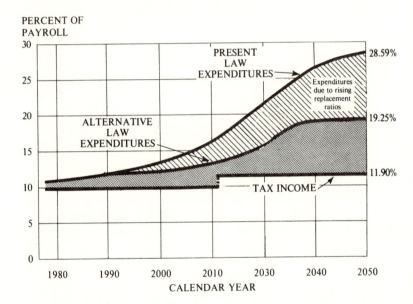

Arithmetic Average of Expenditures, Tax Income, and Deficits under Present Law and Illustrative Alternative Law Expressed as a Percentage of Taxable Payroll

Time Period	Present Law			Illustrative Alternative Law		
	Expenditures	Tax Income	Deficit	Expenditures	Tax Income	Deficit
1976-2000	11.8%	9.90%	1.91%	11.58%	9.90%	1.68%
2001-2025	17.95	11.10	6.85	14.91	11.10	3.81
2026-2050	27.04	11.90	15.14	19.30	11.90	7.40
1976-2050	18.93	10.97	7.96	15.25	10.97	4.28

This more comforting outlook was not, however, the focus of attention—neither the attention of the trustees nor that of Congress nor that of the news media. The focus was on the existing and prospective deficits under the existing law, on the increase in projected future costs over those anticipated in 1975, and on proposals of the Ford administration for an increase in the social security payroll tax.

Some legislators such as Senator Hubert H. Humphrey, then chairman of the Joint Economic Committee of Congress, scolded the trustees for frightening the public; he expressed a fundamental doubt about the validity of the statistical exercise, and perhaps also about the ability of legislators to act wisely for a long-term future.

DEMOGRAPHIC CHANGES, INFLATION, AND DOUBLE INFLATION ADJUSTMENT

There were three reasons why the social security financing picture had turned grim. A falling birthrate meant that in the future there would be fewer persons working and paying the taxes that finance social security benefits. From a post-World War II high of 3.7 children born per woman in 1957, the national fertility rate had fallen to 1.8 in 1976. Demographers at the Social Security Administration estimated that the rate might rise to 1.9 by the year of 2005. Figure 2 shows that because of the declining birthrate, the number of social security beneficiaries for every hundred workers paying social security taxes would climb from 31 in 1976 to more than 50 by the middle of the twenty-first century.[8]

The second cause of the worsened outlook was inflation. For a variety of reasons, inflation in the United States and elsewhere had accelerated in 1973-1974 beyond the expectations of most analysts. By early 1976, even though inflation was decelerating, the managers of the social security program felt they had to anticipate average annual wage increases of 5.75 percent after 1981 and average rises in the Consumer Price Index of 4 percent.[9] Of course, these assumptions are open to dispute.

A third source of the prospective deficits was the 1972 amendment to the Social Security Act that provided for automatic in-

Old Age, Survivors, and
Disability Insurance Program

FIGURE 2

Projected Beneficiaries per Hundred
Covered Workers
1976-2050

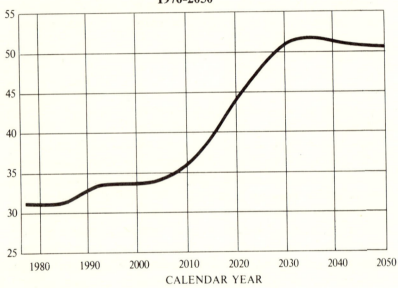

CALENDAR YEAR

PRINCIPAL ASSUMPTIONS

Mortality rates were assumed to decline overall by about 15% from 1976 to 2050.

Fertility rates were assumed to continue decreasing to *1.75 children per women in 1977 and then slowly increase to an ultimate rate of 1.90 children per women in 2005.*

Female labor force participation rates were projected to increase to an ultimate level 22% greater than the 1975 level. The unemployment rate for the total labor force was assumed to be *5% after 1981.*

Disability incidence rates were projected to continue increasing of a level 33% higher than the 1975 level.

Under these assumptions the population would grow from its level of 223 million in mid-1975 to 274 million by the year 2015, remaining slightly above that level through the year 2050.

creases in benefits according to inflation. For those retired, that seemed fair enough. But the amendment also provided that the taxable earnings base would keep step with inflation to provide more tax revenue, and that the formula for calculating the "primary insurance amount" (PIA)—the initial benefit payment to a newly retired person—would increase with the Consumer Price Index. The PIA formula is applied to average monthly earnings as determined by a separate formula. Increasing the earnings base while increasing the PIA formula meant that future retirees would be doubly compensated for inflation, as Alicia Munnell has pointed out.[10]

REPLACEMENT RATIOS

One effect of this coupling of higher covered earnings with a more generous formula for calculating benefits would be to increase replacement ratios, the ratio of benefits to earnings at retirement. (See Figure 3.) Social Security Administration projections showed these ratios rising steadily to the year 2050 for newly retired workers. For low-wage earners ($3,789 in 1975), whose replacement ratios are highest by legislative policy, the projection shows the ratio reaching 112 percent in the year 2050, under the intermediate economic assumptions. Plainly, Congress didn't intend that. Nor did it intend that replacement ratios vary with changing rates of wage and price inflation, as they would do under the 1972 amendment. One must agree with the argument advanced by the Social Security Administration that if future replacement ratios are to be more (or less) generous than now, that change should result from a conscious decision by Congress, not from the vagaries of wage and price movements.[11]

"Decoupling," or eliminating the double adjustment for inflation, is a technical problem that can be solved in more than one way. In 1976 a panel of consultants to Congress recommended that benefits be calculated from "earnings . . . indexed in proportion to the change in price levels during the earnings-averaging period."[12] Decoupling may be the most technically forbidding aspect of the social security crisis, but perhaps the least controversial. No politi-

**Old-Age, Survivors, and Disability
Insurance Program**

FIGURE 3

**Replacement Ratios* for Males Retiring at Age 65
Low, Median and Maximum Wage Earners**
(Intermediate Economic Assumptions)*****

PERCENT

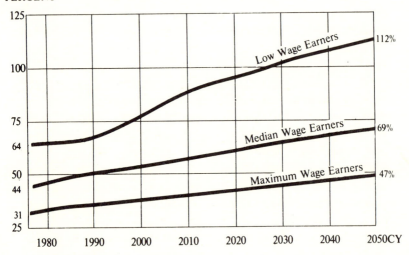

* The Replacement Ratio is the ratio of the initial benefit to the earnings just prior to retirement.

** Low wage earners are defined as workers earning the Federal minimum wage. In 1975 "low", median and maximum earnings were $3,789; $8,188 and $14,100 respectively.

*** The intermediate set of assumptions includes an ultimate CPI annual increase of 4% and an ultimate wage annual increase of 5-3/4%.

cal opposition to decoupling has surfaced. Presumably Congress will get around to it in a year or two or three.

THE LONG-TERM DEFICIT

Even with decoupling, deficits in the social security system loom, as the trustees' "modified theoretical system" showed. What to do about the deficit, in broadest terms, is a question Congress has shied away from. One alternative is to pay it out of the general revenues of the Treasury. Another is to increase social security tax revenues, which could be done in several ways. A third, which would complement either of the others, would be to diminish outlays.

Political realism directs that students of social security policy devote little time and effort to the third alternative. The fundamental issue seems to shape up as one of increasing social security tax revenues versus financing part of social security from the general fund of the Treasury.

The first issue parallels a major theme in the debate on social security and in this book: whether to regard social security as primarily an insurance program of earned benefits, or as a transfer program aimed at social adequacy of benefits. Since its founding the program has always had elements of both. Those like Joseph Pechman, who emphasize the transfer goal, oppose raising the payroll tax rate on grounds that the tax is regressive. It takes a larger percentage of the total income of persons making less than the taxable wage base than of those who make more. In 1977, Pechman calculates, social security taxes "will be the highest tax paid by about two-thirds of the nation's income recipients," including those officially classified as living in poverty.

Others in the book—notably George Break, Kip Viscusi, and Richard Zeckhauser—emphasize the insurance goal. Break and Carl Patton both argue strongly that public attitudes toward the payroll tax depend largely on their continued perception of the program as primarily committed to earned benefits. And Break especially warns against a radical departure from the concept of earned entitlements on grounds that such a move would undermine the program's sense of equity and threaten public support for it.

Interestingly, Milton Friedman sides with Pechman in urging the use of general revenues, as well as a *reduction* in the payroll tax; they come to the same policy recommendations, but for very different reasons.

A tax rise is likely to be a drag on the economy. And while half of any tax increase is paid by employers, a number of authors in the book argue the real economic burden falls entirely on workers.

Another way to increase revenues would be to raise the taxable wage base. However, as the ceiling moves higher on the pyramid of wage earners, the additional revenue yield diminishes. The AFL-CIO has proposed removal of the ceiling altogether for employer contributions, evidently with an eye on stratospheric executive salaries. In the book Martin Feldstein and Sherwin Rosen explore the effects of various alternatives on the overall economy—especially on spending, saving, and investment.

PUBLIC EMPLOYEE WITHDRAWALS

At present federal employees are exempt from participation in social security and have a retirement program of their own. Compelling federal employee participation might increase revenue, and so might prevention of withdrawals by state and local governments. The constitutionality of making state and local participation is not compulsory, it is voluntary; moreover, withdrawal is permitted by a covered group with two years notice. That notice can be rescinded before it takes effect, but once it takes effect, it is irrevocable. Withdrawals have been increasing and continuation of the trend poses a fiscal threat to the old-age trust fund. In fiscal 1975, taxes paid by state and local government workers and their employers amounted to 11 percent of total tax revenues.[13]

Apart from the loss of revenues, withdrawal poses an equity issue. Many employees of state and local governments would be entitled to benefits when they reach retirement age. Indeed, benefits are relatively most generous for those who have paid in least.

How to arrest the trend poses a dilemma. As the *Wall Street Journal* has commented editorially,[14] making participation compulsory—if sustained on constitutional grounds—would lead to dismemberment of state and local pension plans, an important source of funds to the capital markets. Congress could rewrite the law to prohibit future withdrawals, but that would have a draconian flavor to it that probably would be repellent to many members of Congress, to many commentators, and to the public. Discouraging withdrawal by removing uncertainties about the costs and benefits of social security would be a more appealing remedy, albeit one easier said than done.

THE EARNINGS TEST

Surely, one way to make social security more generally attractive would be to remove the earnings test for retirees. In 1977 a beneficiary stood to lose $1 in social security benefits for every $2 he or she earned above $3,000 a year. For years, beneficiaries have complained about the earnings test, perceiving it as an unjust punishment for being willing to work, an activity otherwise applauded by the American ethos. To the person who has "earned" benefits by years of "contributions," a forced choice between working and collecting benefits is seen as unfair. Part of the issue, again, relates to the question of whether social security is essentially a program based on earned entitlements, or on need.

Zeckhauser and Viscusi argue that repeal of the earnings test will lead not to more unemployment of younger persons but to a larger economy. They also argue that removal of the earnings test will encourage the elderly to support themselves, diminishing the burden on public funds. It might be added that removal of the earnings test also would diminish the pressures on Congress to liberalize social security benefits.

OTHER PROBLEMS OF FAIRNESS

The earnings test is one of many problems of fairness that have cropped up as Congress has elaborated social security benefits for workers, spouses, survivors, and children, and as women, especially married women, have increased their tendency to work. Fairness issues, as Rita Ricardo Campbell explains in her chapter in this book, arise from differences in age, marital status, dependents, participation in the labor force, and employment in non-covered jobs such as the federal civil service. Many of these so-called fairness issues may turn on a choice between the insurance goal and the transfer goal. Although less exigent than the financing problem, dealing with these issues too would help to strengthen public confidence in social security.

THE RETIREMENT AGE

When Congress gets around to dealing with the long-term social security deficit, it will find itself confronted by two large issues: the use of general revenues of the Treasury to pay part of the social security bill, and extension of the retirement age. The latter is probably an issue whose time has not yet come. It is unlikely that Congress would be willing to change the retirement age until it had been a topic of public discussion for some years, and then only if a consensus in favor of later retirement was in the air. Deferring retirement would involve a change of thinking and expectations.

People who have contemplated retiring at age 62 or age 65 would have to be given considerable notice that they would have to work longer. Senator Russell Long, chairman of the Senate Finance Committee, believes that retirement should be deferred for several reasons: because the elderly are healthier, because they want to work, because they will probably realize a larger benefit if they work longer, and because it would help ease the financial strains on the social security system. Senator Long has in mind amendments in the 1980s that might not take effect for ten or fifteen years, giving working people time to adjust their plans.[15]

THE LONG-TERM PROSPECT

The long-term social security deficit remains the overriding issue. There is opposition to increases in the payroll tax because of its regressive nature; but the regressivity could be modified by taking account of personal exemptions and low income. The earned income tax credit also could be improved to moderate the regressive effect.

One could imagine that if Congress violates the principle of pay-as-you-go it will turn onto a path from which there would be no turning back. Unless the ratio of workers to beneficiaries takes an unexpected jump at some future time, it is difficult to imagine that an infusion of general revenues would be temporary. It is easier to imagine that Congress would reduce the payroll tax, if only for lower income brackets. It is also easier to imagine that social security would lose its separate identity as general revenues came to account for an ever larger share of benefit payments. Ultimately, integration of the payroll tax with the personal income tax could come about.

The critical, unanswered question is how partial funding from general revenues will affect the public perception of social security—especially the attitudes of employee-taxpayers, who have paid rising payroll taxes in the belief that they were providing for their own futures. How they feel undoubtedly will influence subsequent policy decisions by Congress about the future of social security. Several contributors to this book argue that any substantial funding of social security out of general revenues may threaten public support for the program.

Despite these uncertainties, general fund contributions may well be the next major event in the evolution of this program that cannot stop. How they will affect the program, whether men and women will decide to have larger families, whether inflation will rage or abate—all of these touch the future of social security. How these forces of American life work themselves out will have much to do with the future of social security.

Whatever the outcome, long-term solutions depend on open public discussion of the policy options. This book will provide an important contribution in clarifying issues and identifying alternatives.

IIA

MARTIN FELDSTEIN

SOCIAL SECURITY

History, and the changing economy. The purposes. Adverse effects on capital accumulation. Conclusion.

The basic features of the current social security program were designed in the midst of the Great Depression. Features that were valuable then are inappropriate in the very different economic conditions of the present and the forseeable future. The time has come to reexamine the purpose of social security and then to redesign the form of the program to serve this purpose with the most favorable (or least adverse) side effects.

Two aspects of the depression had a major effect on the design of the social security program. First, the length of the depression and the failure of financial institutions had wiped out the lifetime savings of a great many families. Second, more than 20 percent of the labor force was unemployed. A social security program that paid benefits to retirees would replace lost savings, stimulate consumption, and open the jobs left by the retirees for younger people who were currently unemployed. Moreover, the new Keynesian economics soon stressed that the depression would persist as long as the full-employment rate of savings remained greater than the rate of investment. The fear that an excessive savings rate would cause a permanent depression remained a firm conviction of many leading economists into the 1940s. They argued that, by providing a substitute for private saving, social security would reduce the future saving rate and thus help to promote full employment.

Economic conditions are now very different. The past twenty five years have seen a relatively low average unemployment rate of less than 5 percent. There is a general consensus among economists that much of this 5 percent represents adverse incentives rather than inadequate demand. The "forced" early retirement no longer serves a socially useful purpose. The early fear of excessive savings has now changed to a serious concern about a capital shortage. A social security system designed to reduce saving was appropriate forty years ago but is no longer appropriate.

In this brief comment I will emphasize the reason for having a social security program at the present time. I will also discuss what I believe is a very serious adverse consequence of the current *form* of social security. It should be clear from these remarks that I agree neither with those who regard social security as an unwarranted interference with private choice and should therefore be eliminated, nor with those who consider the current social security program to be a wholly successful and benign institution that can only be improved by raising benefits and making it an instrument of greater income redistribution. I believe instead that a social security program has a valuable role to play, but that the structure of our current program entails harmful side effects which could be remedied by restructuring certain basic features.[1]

The Purpose of Social Security

The valid purpose of social security today is to provide annuities which could not or would not be purchased otherwise. There is, of course, a substantial intellectual difference between a "could not" and a "would not," between correcting an imperfect market and imposing a paternalistic policy. Both deserve more complete discussion.

Everyone who is covered by social security could not buy equivalent annuities on the private insurance market. Of course, insurance companies do sell retirement and disability annuities, and life insurance can provide an annuity for surviving dependents. Although annuities adjusted for inflation to preserve the same real benefits are not currently available, this would be remedied quickly if the government offered to sell price-indexed bonds. Insurance companies can offer annuity policies that are close to being actuarially fair for moderate and large groups. Sizable employers or unions can make a collective purchase of insurance for their members. It is understandable, however, that insurance companies generally cannot sell actuarially fair policies to individuals or very small groups. Adverse selection, i.e., a greater demand for insurance by those with higher expected benefits, forces insurance companies to charge higher premiums for individual coverage than for group coverage. These higher premiums exacerbate the problem of adverse selection, thus causing a further premium increase, etc. Many of those who have no reason to believe that they are high risk cases find the cost of insurance so high that they choose not to insure.

Social security avoids the adverse selection problem by forming one big group. It might reasonably be objected that a compulsory social security system is not necessary to remedy this defect in the market. To permit everyone to buy as much insurance as he currently gets from social security and on the same financial terms, it would only be necessary to offer such insurance on a voluntary basis. Individuals could buy all of their insurance in this way or could supplement group plans that they regard as inadequate. Although the insurance would not be sold at individually actuarially fair rates, the terms would be as good as they are under the current compulsory program. Anyone or any group that found such terms unsatisfactory could either buy commercial insurance or simply remain uninsured.

This brings us to the second purpose of social security, to provide insurance to those who would not otherwise buy it for themselves. Why should the government be so paternalistic as to compel individuals to buy annuity insurance that they would not otherwise choose to buy? I think that there are three distinct reasons. First, if there were no social security it would be necessary to have a welfare program for older people with no other means of support. Such a means-tested program would induce low-income workers to avoid accumulating assets because of the high implicit rate of "tax" implied by such a means-tested grant. When they retire their level of consumption may be lower than it would have been in the absence of a means tested welfare grant. Social security, by providing retirement benefits without regard to wealth, avoids this distortion of saving. In this respect, the desirability of social security depends on balancing the reduced distortions in the saving of this group against the other distortions introduced by social security.

The second rationale for compulsory annuity insurance is the potentially high cost of private choice. Insurance, annuities, and compound interest are all hard concepts for a large part of the population to understand and use correctly. The government might try to educate the public so that every individual could make a well-informed choice. But this would be expensive in terms of both government spending and the time that individuals must spend in learning. If everyone would eventually reach the same conclusion (and therefore a conclusion that the government can anticipate), it would obviously be more efficient to avoid the information and decision-making costs. Of course, such unanimity is most unlikely. But, to the extent that there is agreement among individuals with the same social and economic characteristics, a compulsory program will be more efficient than using the resources to inform individual choices. Since workers with higher earnings are likely to want bigger annuities, there is a justification for the income-related benefits provided by social security. Again, the efficient answer is not clear cut but requires a balancing of opposing considerations. Moreover, libertarians would regard a restriction on individual choice as unjustified by any efficiency gain. And pessimists would regard the variety of individual answers as a safeguard against the imposition of a single answer that is wrong for everyone.

Finally, even if all of the objective information about survival and disability probabilities, interest rates, future incomes, etc., were fully known and fully understood by everyone, some individuals would still make the mistake of giving too much weight to current consumption and not enough to future consumption. If left to their own choice, they would eventually look back with the hindsight of old age and regret that they had not saved more. If everyone were so myopic in his individual decision-making, a benevolent government could raise everyone's lifetime well-being by compelling additional saving. Unless myopia became less important in high income groups, the amount of compulsory saving should increase with income. If, as is more likely, only some individuals are myopic, the appropriate policy would be to require additional saving only if the individual's choice was below a given level. If this is not possible, or if the appropriate saving differs among individuals according to characteristics that the government cannot observe, it is necessary to balance the gain from offsetting insufficient saving against the loss of forcing saving that is too high. Again there are some who will reject these criteria and insist that efficiency gains must be subservient to individual liberty or, at least, that the two must be balanced against each other in reaching this decision.

The Adverse Effect on Capital Accumulation

Although the reasons that I have now discussed may justify requiring individuals to purchase income-related annuities, none of these reasons indicate that the annuities should be provided by the government on a pay-as-you-go basis. The most serious effect of this current method of operating the social security program is to reduce the nation's rate of saving and therefore our rate of capital accumulation. Recall that with our pay-as-you-go method, social security tax receipts are paid out as concurrent benefits and are not accumulated. There is no real investment of social security tax payments, and therefore no interest as such is earned on these compulsory contributions. When we, the current generation of workers, retire, we will not receive social security benefits by drawing down an accumulated fund. Instead our benefits will be financed by the tax payments of those who are at work when we retire.

For most Americans, the social security program is the major form of saving. Consider, for example, an individual with an income of $10,000 who, in the absence of social security, would wish to save 10 percent of his total income for his old age. With social security, such an individual would not have to do any saving at all for his retirement. He need save only to buy consumer durables and to have a cash balance for emergencies. Similarly, an individual with an income of $20,000 who, in the absence of social security, would want to save 10 percent of his income (or $2,000), finds that social security now involves compulsory savings of about $1,800. He would therefore need to save only an additional $200 instead of $2,000.

In 1975, total social security contributions were some $70 billion, or 7 percent of total disposable personal income. If individuals think of these contributions as equivalent to savings and reduce their own personal savings accordingly, the effect on total savings would be very substantial. In 1975 personal savings were $90 billion, or 9 percent of disposable personal income. Of course, not all private savings are personal savings; in 1975, corporate savings were $30 billion. Total private savings were thus $120 billion. If social security did reduce savings by $80 billion, the total potential private savings of $200 billion were reduced by about 40 percent.

Because social security taxes are not actually compulsory savings, but only an exchange of taxes for an implicit promise of future benefits, it is also useful to look at the likely effect of social security on savings in a quite different way. Instead of considering the social security contributions, the individual might focus on his expected benefits. Being covered by social security is like owning an annuity—i.e., a claim on future annual payments when the individual reaches age 65. These implicit social security annuities are an important part of each family's wealth. An individual with such an annuity could reduce his own private accumulation of wealth— whether held directly or through private pensions—by an equal amount.

It is therefore interesting to use the total value of these social security annuities as an estimate of the likely effect of social security on the total private stock of real wealth. In a recent study,[2]

I estimated the 1971 value of this social security "wealth" at $2 trillion.[3] Since the total private wealth of households in that year was about $3 trillion, the calculation suggests that social security may have reduced the stock of private wealth by about 40 percent—i. e., from $5 trillion of wealth that would exist without social security to the $3 trillion that currently exists. The 40 percent reduction is remarkably close to the estimate obtained by looking at the reduction in personal savings that would occur if households viewed social security taxes as an alternative to savings.

The relative importance of social security "wealth" has grown very rapidly in the past two decades. In 1950, social security "wealth" was 88 percent of gross national product. A decade later it had increased to 133 percent of gross national product. Today it is more than 200 percent of gross national product. The impact on capital accumulation is thus more important than ever before.

The potential importance of the effect of social security on capital accumulation has induced economists to undertake a number of detailed statistical studies to measure the size of the actual effect. The general indication of these econometric studies is that social security does substantially reduce such private saving.[4] How does such a reduction in savings affect the American economy? How would our economy be different if the rate of saving were substantially higher? To be specific in my answers, let me use the estimate that social security reduces the nation's rate of saving by about 35 percent. If this asset substitution had not occurred, the long-run capital stock would be significantly higher than it currently is. This would imply that gross national product would rise about 20 percent. For 1975, then, GNP would be increased by more than $285 billion. To put this number in some perspective, note that $285 billion is nearly 30 percent of total consumer spending, more than twice the total of individual income tax payments, and substantially more than twice the level of national defense expenditures. Viewed somewhat differently, $288 billion is $1,300 per person, or more than $3,500 per family. *Let me emphasize that this lower level of GNP reflects the pay-as-you-go nature of our social security system.* It is because social security taxes are used to pay concurrent benefits that the capital stock is smaller and income is less than it would otherwise be.

However, the most important implication of the lower rate of saving is not the fall in income as such. The reduction in our nation's well-being comes rather from substituting a social security program with a very low implicit rate of return in the place of real capital accumulation with a much higher return. Social security cannot hope to provide an implicit "yield" of more than 2 percent a year while additional investment in real plant and equipment would yield the nation some 12 percent a year.

The crucial challenge to social security is therefore to find a way to provide protection for everyone in old age without sacrificing the potential yield on real capital accumulation. One way to do this is to enlarge the role for private pension programs. The other is to develop a substantial capital fund for the public social security program.[5] It should be clear that the long-run level of the social security benefits should be influenced by the extent to which it is possible to have high benefits without an adverse effect on capital accumulation.

CONCLUSION

Although we do not yet know enough to predict precisely how individuals will respond to different combinations of social security benefits and financing, we can begin to understand and quantify these effects. On the basis of such an understanding, we can start the important task of redesigning the social security program for the economic conditions of the present and the future. Only if programs are reexamined and redefined in this way can their good features be strengthened while their adverse consequences are reduced.

IIB

MILTON FRIEDMAN

PAYROLL TAXES, NO; GENERAL REVENUES, YES

Social security myths: "contributions," the "trust fund," and the insurance myth. Regressivity of the payroll tax. Capriciousness of benefits. Imaginative packaging and the growth of government. "Fiscal conservatives" and the myth of social security. Conservative cooption by "big spenders." The broader problem. The importance of reducing the payroll tax and of general revenue finance. Reform and changing public perceptions.

A widely circulated booklet, *Your Social Security,* put out by the U.S. Department of Health, Education and Welfare, begins its section on "Financing":

> The basic idea of social security is a simple one: during working years employees, their employers, and self-employed people pay social security contributions into special trust funds. When earnings stop or are reduced because the worker retires, dies, or becomes disabled, monthly cash benefits are paid to replace part of the earnings the family has lost.[2]

It would be hard to pack a greater number of false and misleading statements into a single paragraph. "Contributions" implies a voluntary payment; but what "employes, their employers, and self-employed people" pay are taxes levied on payrolls. Moreover, "employers" do not pay them in any sense other than that in which retail stores may be said to "pay" sales taxes. The tax, whether nominally paid by the worker or the employer, is borne by the worker. His employer simply transmits the amount.

"Into special trust funds" implies that the taxes paid in are accumulated to pay later benefits. This is, of course, not true. The "special trust funds" are small, currently about $56 billion, and consist simply of promises by one branch of government to pay another branch. The present value of pensions already promised to persons covered by social security (both those who have retired and those who have not yet done so) is estimated as totalling several trillions of dollars. That is the size of the trust fund that would justify the words of the booklet.

The paragraph gives the impression—though it does not literally say so—that a worker's "benefits" are financed by his own "contributions" out of the pooled "trust funds." That impression is wholly false. Current benefits to persons already retired are being paid from current taxes being collected from persons at work. The so-called "trust fund" could more accurately be termed a "petty cash" fund.

What assurance do current workers have that they will receive the benefits promised? Solely the confidence that our children will be willing to impose taxes on themselves to pay benefits being promised by us to ourselves. this one-sided "compact between the generations," foisted on generations that literally cannot give their consent, may be sufficient assurance, but it is a very different thing from a "trust fund"—a "chain letter" would be a more accurate designation.

The booklet goes on: "Nine out of ten working people in the United States are now building protection for themselves and their families under the social security program."

More doublethink.

What nine out of ten working people are now doing is paying

taxes to finance benefits to persons who are not working. An individual working person is in no sense building his own protection—as a person who contributes to a private vested pension system is building his own protection. Persons now receiving benefits are receiving much more than the actuarial value of the taxes that were paid on their behalf. Young persons are now being promised much less than the actuarial value of the taxes that are being paid on their behalf.

More fundamentally yet, the relationship between taxes paid and benefits received is extremely loose. Millions of people will never receive any benefits attributable to their taxes because they have not paid for enough quarters to qualify, or because they receive benefits as spouses rather than on their own account. Two persons may receive the same benefit, yet may have very different taxes over their working lives because they worked different numbers of years. Conversely, two persons may have paid precisely the same taxes at the same times, yet may receive very different benefits because one is married and the other is single. A man who continues working after age 65 will be required to pay additional taxes, yet may receive no benefits at all.

Social security is not in any meaningful sense an insurance program in which individual payments purchase equivalent actuarial benefits. It is a combination of a tax—a flat-rate tax on wage income up to a maximum—and a program of transfer payments, in which all sorts of considerations other than the amount paid determine the amount received.

Taken by itself, the payroll tax is almost surely the most regressive element in our tax system. For most families of low or modest income, it is by far the heaviest tax they bear. Its inequity is compounded by its disincentive effects: simultaneously discouraging employers from hiring workers and potential workers from accepting jobs by driving a substantial wedge between the wage cost to the employer and the net return to the worker.

Taken by itself, the benefits are capricious and inequitable. Surely a sensible benefit system would try to relate the benefits to some criteria of "need" and the availability of other resources. It would not make benefits depend on whether the recipient worked in a covered or noncovered industry, or how long he had worked and at what wages, etc. It would not completely disregard the wealth of the recipient or his income—if that income does not come from work. (There are millionaires who regularly receive social security; and it is entirely legal for them to do so, so long as their ample annual income derives from returns on investments and not from current employment.)

Hardly any student of social security—or, more broadly, hardly anyone, whatever his social and political views—would approve of either the tax separately, or the benefit system separately; yet the two, combined, have become a sacred cow. I know of no greater triumph of imaginative packaging and Madison Avenue advertising.

The imaginative packaging has served a very important political function: it has made the public at large willing to pay much heavier taxes than they otherwise would have been willing to bear; it has made them willing to accept a capricious system of benefits and to support a mammoth bureaucracy that could never have arisen separately. The ultimate effect has been to foster the growth of government and, above all, of central government.

Perhaps the most striking example of the potency of the imaginative packaging is the success it has had in converting self-styled "fiscal conservatives" into willing allies of those whom they would term "big spenders." The obvious financial problems of social security led President Ford to propose a further increase in the payroll tax, and this proposal was hailed by many "fiscal conservatives" as courageous fiscal procedure.

In my opinion it was precisely the reverse. True fiscal conservatism calls for holding down government spending, not cooperating in its growth. Yet by accepting the myth that social security is an insurance program in which there is a valid connection between taxes and spending, President Ford's approach simply enhances the willingness of the public to pay taxes and, in this way encourages the growth of government.

The point at issue is part of a much broader problem—the tendency for fiscal conservatives to stress the deficit rather than government spending. I believe, along with Parkinson, that government will spend whatever the explicit tax system will raise—plus a good deal more. The historical process has been that government spending has raced ahead of explicit taxes, producing a deficit. Fiscal conservatives, alarmed by the deficit, proceeded to cooperate in enacting taxes to close the deficit. The result: a further burst of spending, and a repetition of the process.

The true cost of government is not measured by explicit taxes, but by total spending. If the federal government spends $450 billion and takes in $380 billion in explicit taxes, who pays the difference? Not Santa Claus but the U.S. citizen. The deficit must be financed by creating money or by borrowing from the public. In either case, a hidden tax is imposed—in the form either of inflation or of the present value of the higher taxes that will be required in the future.

This line of reasoning has led me to favor tax reduction under any and all circumstances, and to oppose tax increases under any and all circumstances, as the only way to bring effective pressure on holding down government spending.

To return to social security, this line of reasoning is reinforced by my conviction that the social security system is an undesirable and inequitable system. It cannot be abolished outright—on both moral and political grounds. Morally, we have entered into commitments to millions of persons who have shaped their lives in accordance with those commitments. We should discharge those commitments, so far as we can do so without imposing still greater inequities on others. Politically, the "chain letter" character of social security has not yet become clearly apparent. Anything that promotes a public understanding of the true character of social security will hasten the day when real reform will be possible.

On these grounds, I oppose any increase in the employment taxes and, indeed, favor any decrease. If revenue from the payroll tax is inadequate to finance current benefits, the difference should be financed from the general Treasury. This will have two advantages: first, it will help to dissolve the public belief, so carefully and dishonestly fostered by the social security bureaucracy, that social security is an insurance system; second, it will absorb funds that would otherwise be available for even more undesirable government programs, such as national health insurance.

This is, of course, only a temporary expedient. For the longer run, we should press for a fundamental reform of our whole set of welfare measures, including social security. I have elsewhere outlined in some detail the direction which I believe such a reform should take.[3]

IIC

JOSEPH A. PECHMAN

THE SOCIAL SECURITY SYSTEM: AN OVERVIEW*

Social security as social insurance. Program expansion since 1935. Regressivity of payroll tax. Proposed reforms. General revenue financing. Trust funds and inflation. Effect on personal savings. Payroll tax and income tax adjustments.

The social security system is perhaps the most successful social program ever enacted by the U.S. government. In a typical month in 1976 it provided about $6 billion of benefits to 32 million retired and disabled people and their dependents and survivors. For most of these people, social security is the major source of income. While poverty among the aged has not been eliminated, social security has brought this goal within reach. Yet despite its success social security of late has been subject to great criticism, and radical

*The views in this paper do not necessarily reflect those of the officers, directors, or other staff members of the Brookings Institution. I am grateful to Henry J. Aaron, John A. Britain, and John L. Palmer for their helpful comments and suggestions.

changes are often suggested for problems that either do not exist or can easily be resolved. This paper will explain the program's rationale and suggest methods of improvement which will not alter its basic character.

RATIONALE OF SOCIAL SECURITY

When the social security program was enacted in 1935, considerable emphasis was placed on its resemblance to private insurance: "contributions" were to be paid by the worker and the employer into a trust fund; interest was credited on trust fund balances; and benefits were formally based on the worker's previous earnings. This emphasis promoted public acceptance of the system as a permanent government institution.

The insurance analogy no longer applies to the system as it has developed. Present beneficiaries as a group receive far larger benefits than the taxes they have paid plus a reasonable rate of return, and new beneficiaries will continue to get a "good deal" as long as Congress keeps benefits in line with higher prices. Although the trust fund balances have tended to increase over the long run, they are rarely large enough to finance more than one year's benefits; payroll taxes paid by workers are not stored up or invested, but are paid out currently as benefits. When the benefits promised to people now working become due, they will be paid from the tax revenues of that future date. Social security thus is really a compact between the working and nonworking generations—a compact which amendments to the basic program have continually renewed and strengthened.

Under this concept, payroll taxes are not insurance premiums; rather they are a financing mechanism for a large, essential, government program. As such, payroll taxes should be evaluated like any other major tax of the federal government. Increases in benefits and expansion of the social security program should not be financed automatically by higher payroll taxes as they have been in the past, but by the best tax source or sources available to the federal government. On the other hand, since benefits are related to past wages, many believe that the system has sufficient insurance elements to justify taxation of payrolls to finance it. But this rationale does not, in my view, preclude the possibility of improving the payroll tax so that it is not a heavy burden on the poor and on low-income workers.

REGRESSIVITY OF THE PAYROLL TAX

Payroll taxes have a significant impact on the tax payments of the lowest income groups. In 1977 the employee and employer taxes for social security, disability, and hospital care will reach 11.7 percent of wages up to $16,500. Most economists believe that the tax on the employer as well as that on the employee is borne by the workers. Thus we extract a payroll tax of $585 from an individual with a family of four and an income of $5,000, even though he is officially classified as poor by the federal government. In return, this worker will receive generous benefits, but these will be deferred for decades.

The payroll tax exceeds the 1977 federal income tax liabilities for single persons with incomes of $13,000, married persons with incomes of $15,000, and married persons (including working couples) with two children and incomes of $17,000. In 1977 the federal payroll tax for OASDHI (Old Age, Survivors, Disability and Hospital Insurance) purposes will be the highest tax paid by about two-thirds of the nation's income recipients, and $2.5 billion will be paid by persons officially classified as living in poverty. This compares with the total cash income poverty gap of about $13 billion.

To moderate the burden of the social security tax on low incomes, in 1975 Congress introduced a refundable income tax credit of 10 percent of family earnings up to $4,000 (phasing down to zero at $8,000) for persons with children. (The credit is "refundable," because cash payments are made to those whose credit exceeds their federal income tax liability or who are not subject to tax.) About 85 percent of the payroll tax liability ($10 \div 11.7$) is eliminated for those who are eligible for the full amount of the credit, but only a minority of workers at those earnings levels are eligible.

A major share of the burden of the payroll tax at the lower end of the income scale would be eliminated if the 10 percent tax credit were increased to the 11.7 percent social security tax rate, and if individuals without children were made eligible for the credit. The cost of such an expanded credit would be about $6 billion a year.

Another possibility would be to introduce into the payroll tax a system of personal exemptions and low-income allowances similar to those used in the individual income tax, and to eliminate the maximum taxable earnings ceiling. This would make the payroll tax a progressive tax on earnings even if there were only a single tax rate. The exemption and low-income allowance would eliminate taxes paid by earners who are below the poverty levels and, without a taxable earnings limit, an increasing proportion of earnings would be taxed as earnings rose.

Still another possibility would be to use existing receipts from the general fund of the Treasury when additional funds are required to finance benefits. Since the general fund relies primarily on progressive taxes, this would automatically improve the equity of the overall tax system.

One way to introduce general revenue financing would be to adopt the recommendation of the 1975 Quadrennial Advisory Council on Social Security that payroll tax receipts of the hospital insurance fund be gradually shifted to the old-age and survivors's insurance fund and that general revenue receipts be used to replace the payroll tax receipts in the hospital fund. The council pointed out that the benefits under the hospital program for the aged are not related to wages, and consequently there is no justification for using a payroll tax to finance these benefits.

None of the methods of moderating or eliminating the regressivity of the social security payroll tax would necessarily require a change in the method of calculating benefits. Benefits are now related to past earnings, not to taxes paid. Since the system's basic objective is to moderate the earnings decline at retirement, the relationship between benefits and past earnings can be preserved whatever the structure of the tax used to finance benefits. Under the present system, benefits are equal to a fraction of average earnings (up to the taxable ceiling). The higher the average earnings, the lower the fraction.

A ceiling on benefits is appropriate because the national retirement system should be used to guarantee benefits on the basis of earnings up to some reasonable level—beyond which private pension arrangements and personal savings can be expected to take over. Expansion of the earned income credit or use of general revenues for financing future revenue needs would not require any change in the method of calculating benefits, since the present payroll tax and the earnings ceiling would be retained. The decision to eliminate entirely the earnings ceiling would require an explicit decision on the point at which earnings replacement would terminate.

CONDITION OF THE TRUST FUNDS

The major purpose of the social security trust funds is to assure the American people that benefits will be paid at the statutory rates, without new Congressional authorization, even if payroll tax receipts for a brief period do not cover current benefits. But the trust funds are not intended for any extended period during which benefits substantially exceed taxes plus interest income. The funds grew to $48.2 billion on 30 June 1975, or to about two-thirds of the outlays of these funds in fiscal year 1976. Since mid-1975 the balances have declined; they are expected to decline for several more years. This decline will be due partly to the declining trend of real wages and partly to the severity of the 1974-1975 recession and the slow rate of the subsequent recovery. If the unemployment rate were, say, at 5 percent, the retirement fund would be running a surplus at the present time. (The disability fund will run increasing deficits in the future because of the long-term upward trend in disability. This problem is beyond the scope of this brief paper.)

In other words, the retirement trust fund acts as an automatic stabilizer and helps economic recovery. Proposals have been made to offset this effect by an increase in the payroll tax rate, but when unemployment rates are higher than desired such action would defeat the purpose of the trust fund and also retard recovery.

Aside from its effect on the rate of economic recovery, a payroll tax rate increase would raise prices. The employer share of the proposed increase would be reflected in costs and would tend to increase the average price level by the amount of the increase—or more, if it is pyramided. Such an effect is quite consistent with the fact that the real tax burden is borne fully by workers.

As long as inflation is higher than desired, the government should be seeking methods of reducing costs rather than increasing them. In this particular instance, costs would be increased even though there is no economic reason to do so.

One way to resolve the problem posed by the declining trust fund balances would be to adopt the recommendation, mentioned earlier, by the Advisory Council on Social Security gradually to shift the payroll tax receipts of the hospital insurance fund to OASDI (Old-Age, Survivors and Disability Insurance) and replace these receipts out of general revenues. No further tax increases beyond those already scheduled should be needed until well into the twenty-first century, when individuals who were born during the period of high birthrates in the 1950s and 1960s will be retiring.

Perhaps the most urgent change that needs to be made to prevent the cost of social security from rising excessively is to revise the method of correcting benefits for inflation. The present formula computes benefits on the basis of nominal earnings and also corrects them for the rise in the consumer price index. Since earnings tend to reflect changes in prices, there is a double adjustment for inflation. Unless corrected promptly, the financial burden of this error will ultimately require inordinately large tax increases or benefit reductions to balance the receipts and outlays of the program.

The over-indexing for inflation can be eliminated in one of two ways. The first would permit social security benefits to continue to grow at the same rate as money wages, thus preserving the present replacement rate—i.e., the ratio of initial retirement benefits to the final wage. An alternative, put forth by a consultant panel of experts to Congress, would have the automatic growth of benefits proceed at the same rate as that of prices instead of money wages. Under this plan real benefits would remain the same but replacement rates would fall, and Congress would be relied upon to make ad hoc upward adjustments if it wishes. In view of the expected bulge of retirees in the next century, it would be prudent to take the latter approach.

EFFECT ON SAVING

Social security provides protection against loss of income resulting from retirement, death, and disability. Before these programs were enacted, individual savings were the only protection against such hazards. Social security may encourage individuals to set aside a smaller amount of personal saving on the ground that a major reason for saving has now been removed. On the other hand, the availability of social security provides an incentive for individuals to retire earlier, and this encourages them to save more.

Thus far these tendencies have probably offset one another and, on balance, total personal saving has not been greatly affected. In fact, personal saving rose from 5.0 to 7.8 percent of disposable income between 1929 and 1975, but many other factors have had a significant influence on the saving ratio. However, the effect of earlier retirement has been virtually exhausted (except for the trend toward early retirement at age 62), so that the incentive to save less because of the existence of social security may predominate in the future.

Some economists argue that the rate of saving is already too low in the United States, and urge that the nation should save more by raising the social security payroll tax in order to accumulate large balances in the trust funds. It is alleged that this saving, if invested in private capital, would be a "good deal" for the worker because the rate of return would be high—as much as 12 percent by some estimates. The data used to buttress this position are rates of return on corporate investment which are by no means indicative of the yield on all private capital. Corporate capital accounts for less than 50 percent of the private capital stock; the remainder consists of dwelling units, farm and nonfarm capital of the noncorporate sector, and land. The rate of return on the entire private capital stock has averaged substantially less than 12 percent in recent years, even if recession years are omitted.

Furthermore, in arguing that large amounts of additional saving will yield high rates of return, these economists ignore the elementary economic point that a large increase in the private capital stock is likely to encounter diminishing returns. It would be unwise to assume that new investment can continue to earn high rates of return regardless of how much saving is pushed into the corporate sector.

There is in any case no compelling logic for assigning the responsibility for additional saving to social security, other than the pragmatic judgment that Congress will not support large government surpluses unless they are to be associated with social security. This judgment would be acceptable if increased reliance on payroll taxes were desirable and a build-up of large surpluses in the federal budget were appropriate.

An across-the-board increase in individual income tax rates of about 1.1 percentage points would raise as much revenue as a percentage point of the payroll tax. When this progressive alternative is available, advocacy of the payroll tax as a method of financing is difficult to understand.

Furthermore, it is doubtful that a vast increase in the supply of saving can be absorbed without unhappy economic repercussions. The record since the end of World War II is by no means reassuring. The economy operated at or near full employment for only brief periods when the nation was not at war (1947-1948, 1955-1957, 1965, and 1973). The rest of the time there was a shortage of demand, not a shortage of saving; in present and immediately foreseeable circumstances we are having the same problem. A precipitate increase in the budget surplus is likely to plunge the nation into a real depression. It would therefore be unwise to increase the saving rate substantially before the economy moves closer to full employment. Even at that stage, the transition to a higher saving rate would have to be managed carefully to maintain an adequate growth in total demand.

CONCLUSIONS

Payroll taxes paved the way for the enactment of a comprehensive system of social security that protects workers against income losses due to retirement and disability. Although the programs were originally described as social insurance, they have substantial non-insurance components that are strongly supported by the public. Even if payroll taxes continue to be the basic method of financing the program, the effects of these taxes on the distribution of income can no longer be ignored. Improvement of the earned income tax credit, introduction of personal exemptions and a low income allowance into the payroll tax, and removal of the maximum taxable earnings ceiling, or use of the general fund for financing increased social security benefits, would improve the equity of these taxes.

The balances in the trust funds have declined since mid-1975 and will continue to decline so long as unemployment remains high. Increases in payroll tax rates to restore these balances would reduce demand and thus make it more difficult to restore prosperity. Increases would also raise employer costs and aggravate the tendency of prices to rise in the face of high unemployment and low capacity utilization rates.

The major financial problem is the heavy cost that will be imposed on the system by the over-adjustment of benefits for inflation. This over-adjustment should be corrected promptly. The costs of the system will also rise dramatically when the people born in the baby boom following the second World War retire, but this problem can be resolved by guaranteeing for the future constant real benefits rather than constant replacement rates.

Claims that the social security system has reduced national saving are exaggerated. If it turns out that more saving by the federal government will be needed in the future, the necessary revenues should be drawn from the general funds of the Treasury which come mainly from the progressive income taxes. Increased payroll taxation would be the worst possible solution.

III

W. KIP VISCUSI   RICHARD ZECKHAUSER

THE ROLE OF
SOCIAL SECURITY
IN INCOME MAINTENANCE*

Sources of retirement income. Government expenditures on directed transfers Social security structure. Earnings to benefits ratio. Intergenerational resource transfer. Savings, insurance, pensions, and social security. Payroll tax inefficiencies and disincentives. Labor force participation rates. Analysis of the earnings test. Demographic projections and future social security burdens.

INTRODUCTION

Social security is the principal program for assisting the elderly. This analysis examines its justification as an income support program, and assesses its effectiveness in assisting its target population. We shall argue that social security does fulfill a valuable mission, although there are obvious defects in its present structure.

---

*This paper is distilled from Viscusi and Zeckhauser (forthcoming).

Until recently, social security enjoyed a favorable reputation, particularly when judged in comparison with other government income support programs. But critics now carp from many quarters. Conservatives complain that, as a coerced savings program, social security both infringes on individual freedom and generates inefficiencies by imposing choices that individuals would not make for themselves.[1] Liberals, joined by an occasional conservative, attack its perceived regressive structure—the ceiling on income subject to the payroll tax; and the benefit structure, which favors those who have earned more in the past and ignores present unearned income.[2] Most recently, some economists have blamed the pay-as-you-go nature of social security for depressing the savings rate for our society (Feldstein 1974). We shall not dwell on these important issues here, in part because we believe they can be remedied by reforming the social security program and by policy changes in other areas, particularly taxation. This analysis will focus on policy recommendations relating to social security's role as an income support program.

THE PRESENT PATTERN OF ASSISTANCE TO THE ELDERLY

Total Levels of Support

Social security contributes impressively to the financing of an individual's elderly years. Average monthly benefit levels in 1975 (the last year for which data are available) were $205 for retirees and $96 for their spouses.[3] Since 1975 benefits have increased with the cost of living; in July 1976 average benefits were $236. Benefit levels depend on past earnings (positively) and earnings in elderly years (negatively). The maximum in monthly benefits a worker could receive in 1975 was $316.50; for 1977 the figure was raised to $422.40.

Social security has traditionally been viewed as a source of replacement income for the elderly. In 1972 the ratio of the social security primary insurance amount (the benefits a fully insured single retiree receives) to earnings in the year before retirement was .45 for low-earnings workers and .32 for all private industrial workers.[4] The relatively greater support for less affluent individuals seems to be appropriate, since they can draw on fewer alternative income sources in financing their old age.

The low replacement rate for all workers (averaging only a third of their pre-retirement income) overstates the income loss associated with retirement. The increase in leisure accompanying retirement enables many individuals to substitute uncompensated personal labor for previous expenditures on market-traded goods and services. Moreover, the loss of income makes many elderly individuals eligible for a range of in-kind aid programs. Finally, the elderly have a variety of other income sources that provide considerably more income than does social security.

Table 1 shows that, depending on the type of houshold unit, social security provides from 30 to 40 percent of the money income for the average elderly household. The program plays a smaller role for married couples than for individuals, because the per capita income for couples is larger and their range of alternative sources of income is broader.*

Besides social security, only earnings and income from assets contribute more than 10 percent of any group's income. Perhaps most striking is the small role played by personal contributions, which provide 2 percent of the income of unmarried women and less than 0.5 percent of the income for elderly couples and unmarried men; contributions would play a somewhat more significant role if in-kind aid were included.

Social security is a partial substitute for the retirement income which would be contributed to, or earned or saved by, the elderly in the program's absence. This suggests that, were there no social security, the figures for these alternative sources of income would be greater in absolute terms. It is difficult to estimate just how much greater they would be. (Sherwin Rosen elaborates this point elsewhere in this volume.)

---

*Elderly couples tend to be younger for two reasons: because they may include one pre-elderly spouse, and because they are younger than their unmarried survivors, widows and widowers. The tendency of employment to decline with age explains much of the earnings disparity between married and unmarried elderly. Whereas married couples derive almost as much income from earnings as from retirement benefits, unmarried individuals receive about three times more retirement than earnings income.

Table 1

Percentage Distribution of Money Income for Aged Units, 1967

Source of Money Income	Married Couples[a]	Unmarried Men	Unmarried Women
Earnings	39	17	14
Retirement benefits:			
OASDHI	30	40	39
Other public pensions	6	10	7
Private group pensions	6	6	2
Total retirement benefits	42	56	48
Veterans benefits	3	5	4
Public assistance	2	5	8
Income from assets	13	14	19
Personal contributions	(b)	(b)	2
Other sources	2	2	4

Source: Bixby (1970, p. 10).

[a] A couple is defined to be a married elderly couple if at least one of the spouses is aged 65 or over.

[b] 0.5 percent or less.

The general character of financing for old age is clear-cut. The elderly provide significantly for themselves through earnings, assets, and retirement benefits. The large role played by assets and earnings casts doubt on the argument that social security imposes an inefficiently high level of savings on individuals. The importance of income from assets is all the more impressive since market imperfections as well as our tax system discourage individuals who wish to provide for their own old age.

The impressive benefit levels for social security may understate the program's worth to those covered. Unlike most household assets, such as bond or corporate stock investments, social security has an annuity function which, in effect, insures against a life span of uncertain duration. Given that actuarially fair annuities are not available, risk-averse individuals will value social security much more highly than its mere expected return, which is roughly comparable to that yielded by private investments.[5] Conservative critics of the program frequently suggest that it should be subsumed under some form of negative income tax. For all but low-income individuals such a policy would sacrifice the insurance aspect of social security—an assured income of earned benefits in each year of life.

Social Security and the Elderly Aid Mix

Excessive government expenditures on directed transfers can pose problems for the intended beneficiaries—here, the elderly. There are several dangers. Since society's total willingness to support any particular group is limited, directed transfers compete with cash assistance efforts. Welfare budgets in many jurisdictions are now substantially smaller than expenditures for medical care of the poor.[6] Moreover, experience with such programs as Medicaid, manpower training programs, and low-income housing shows enormous potential for inefficiency in directed transfer programs. Unfortunately, public hostility toward nonaccomplishment, fraud, and waste is often directed at the target group rather than the policymakers who misformulated the program, or the administrators who ran it poorly. Among directed transfer programs for elderly assistance, care in nursing homes is most suspiciously regarded. Because of this, such care may threaten the generosity of support for programs of more general assistance to the elderly, including social security.

Fortunately, the total pattern of assistance for the elderly has not evolved to a point where it disproportionately favors directed transfers, although there is a danger in the funding structure for elderly programs. General revenues contribute to all but social security. Since increases in the payroll tax supporting social security are highly visible, political forces may make it easier to increase other, directed areas of expenditure on behalf of the elderly. Medicare—by far the largest directed program and the greatest threat as a wasteful effort—has strong theoretical justifications as insurance, particularly since society undoubtedly would spend equivalent monies for the medical needs of many elderly without Medicare. Unlike most other programs of medical assistance to the poor, Medicare wisely contains deductibles and coinsurance provisions in an effort to limit demand.

Though social security and Medicare have received most attention, several government agencies have other assistance programs targeted at the elderly, including the Foster Grandparent Program, the food stamp program, manpower programs, Department of Transportation demonstration grant programs, and ten HUD housing programs. Cash grant efforts are equally diverse.

Table 2 summarizes the major breakdowns of cash and service programs for FY 1973, the latest year for which detailed information is available.[7] Services and other in-kind aid to the elderly totaled $13.13 billion, of which the largest component—$9.09 billion—went to Medicare. Cash transfers of $45.33 billion exceeded in-kind aid by more than a factor of three. By far the largest of these income transfer programs was social security, which awarded $33.03 billion to the elderly. Most other cash transfers came from retirement programs for individuals not covered by social security—civil service workers, railroad employees, veterans, and the elderly poor. Overall, cash transfers accounted for 77.5 percent of all elderly assistance in FY 1973; 56.5 percent were social security benefits to the elderly.

Updated estimates would show a substantial role—roughly $5.8 billion per year—for Supplemental Security Income (SSI). SSI is a new program, administered by the Social Security Administration, to provide cash grants to the indigent elderly who were formerly served by state-run income support programs, and to railroad and military people not covered by social security.[8]

Table 2

A Profile of Elderly Aid Programs

Agency or Program	FY 1973 Budget (in millions)	
	Sample Specific Programs	Total Government Agency
SERVICES AND RESTRICTED CASH GRANTS		
Civil Service Commission		$ 76.05
Action		40.00
Dept. of Agriculture		412.50
Food Stamp Program	$ 299.10	
Dept. of Transportation		2.49
Dept. of Labor		19.70
Dept. of Housing and Urban Development		563.72
Low-Rent Public Housing	388.50	
Veterans Administration		617.86
Veterans Hospitalization	401.07	
Office of Economic Opportunity		100.82
Dept. of Health, Education, and Welfare		11,296.72
PHS-SRS Medical Asistance for Aged	1,637.00	
PHS-SRS Social Services	224.00	
PHS-SRS Development of		
Programs for the Aging	200.99	
SSA Hospital Insurance Payments	6,645.00	
SSA Supplementary Medical		
Insurance Payments	2,445.00	_____
TOTAL SERVICES AND RESTRICTED CASH GRANTS		$13,129.86
CASH TRANSFERS TO THE ELDERLY		
Civil Service Commission (Retirement		
and Disability Fund)		$4,293.42
Dept. of Defense		515.50
Dept. of Labor (Unemployment Insurance)		281.60
Dept. of Transportation (Coast		
Guard Retirement Pay)		10.23
Veterans Administration		2,520.00
Railroad Retirement Board (Retirement Benefits)		2,102,00
Dept. of Health, Education, and Welfare		
Retirement/Survivors Insurance Payments	33,032.00	
Grants to States for Maintenance Insurance	1,224.44	_____
TOTAL CASH TRANSFER		$45,325.63
TOTAL AID TO THE ELDERLY		$58,455.49

An Overview of the Structure of Social Security

The basic structure of social security has remained unchanged since its inception. Workers are taxed to fund the benefits for the current elderly population. In the Great Depression when the program was founded, this was the only conceivable means of operating, since a lump-sum initial endowment was out of the question. The social security program at the outset was designed to support an impoverished group—thereby putting purchasing power into the economy—and to remove the elderly from the shrunken labor force to make room for younger workers.[9]

In contrast, today the program's primary purpose is to transfer resources from the relatively affluent working population to the relatively poor elderly beneficiaries. The program could be—and indeed has been—justified as a means of letting all individuals in society benefit from an expanding population and growing productivity. Basically, the program is like a chain letter, with successive generations serving as the next round of letter recipients. Recent declines in the birthrate and in productivity growth reduce the attractiveness and security of such a scheme, at least in the short run, though the increased entrance of women into the labor force may offset losses to the base of support.

Social security also has distributional consequences within an age group. The employee payroll tax consists of an 11.7 percent tax on the first $16,500 of income, with the tax split between employer and employee. The division of the tax is economically irrelevant—except perhaps in collective bargaining contexts, where labels may matter, or if other institutional constraints which make wage determination noncompetitive. It is the combined tax contribution that is important. Because of a falsely perceived relationship between the paying and bearing of the tax, the framers of the social security program decided to split the difference in setting the tax rate for self-employed individuals; their 7.9 percent rate is discriminatorily favorable. The lowest average taxes are paid by individuals with incomes well above the $16,500 ceiling, and the self-employed—a category that includes many high-income professionals

But to assess the distributional consequences of social security we must consider the structure of benefits as well as costs. Benefits are positively related to past earnings, but at a less than proportional rate. This pattern in itself is not fully informative. To assess the degree of progressivity of social security, we would have to look at lifetime-earnings profiles for different classes of individuals. The profiles would include statistics on entry and exit from the labor force and on mortality rates, to determine how likely and for how long individuals will receive benefits in their elderly years. Appropriate calculations require data not presently available.

Extrapolating by the use of econometric techniques, Aaron (1974) compared the ratio of discounted expected benefits to discounted expected costs for various groups in the population. For most workers, the high-income earners tended to reap the greatest expected benefit per dollar contributed. Married white males, for example, have an expected social security benefit/cost ratio of .95 if they have not completed grade school, and 1.15 if they have completed at least four years of college. Since the ratio's denominator is greater for the high earners, a look to absolute benefits would show an even more regressive pattern. Nonwhites show a different pattern. Because the benefit/cost ratio tends to decline with years of education in all categories considered, the highest benefit/cost ratio observed in any race/marital status group is 1.49, which goes to married nonwhites who have completed 9-11 years of education. We have found no calculations imputing the cost to an individual of curtailing work, or even retiring altogether, in order to qualify for benefits. This imputed cost should, of course, be included.

Social security has been severely criticized for its regressive structure. Proposals for reform most often recommend that contributions be made more progressive. Steps in this direction include removing the income ceiling on contributions, or financing social security out of general tax revenues.[10]

We do not agree that social security should be changed to ensure progressive distributional consequences. Social security is but one of many instruments—including primarily transfer programs and the tax structure—that the society employs to redistribute income. While it is appropriate to ask that the overall structure of government benefits and costs be progressive, we should not demand that of each component program. Indeed, it could be argued that many of the past decade's most wasteful government efforts have attempted to promote redistribution through programs not well tailored to that purpose. If the total mix of government programs is to be efficient in redistributing resources—if, in effect, the mix is to provide the greatest benefits to the poor at any given level of cost for the rest of society—then across all programs the trade-off between benefits to different interest groups must be the same. To assure a constant trade-off, programs that are effective in promoting net benefits predominantly for the middle classes should specialize in that activity. Such programs would be complemented, of course, by programs that were most effective in helping the poor. That social security is not entirely progressive in its structure would be more disturbing if there were evidence that it could be made an effective instrument of income redistribution.

Proposals have been made to turn social security into a tool of redistribution within generations. The most persistent recommendation is that benefits be funded in part from general revenues. This would undoubtedly inject new political considerations into a system that has worked well in the past. Such tampering might also destroy one of social security's most attractive aspects: the widespread belief that it is a system whereby, on an actuarial basis, individuals provide for their own old age. The persistence of this myth helps social security to maintain its positive image and contributes to the dignity of social security recipients.

Transferring resources to the elderly is social security's dominant redistributional accomplishment. Those most concerned about distribution should not forget that social security contributes the largest proportion of family income for those elderly who were formerly poor. Moreover, it is complemented by many specific aid efforts such as the SSI program, Medicaid, and food stamps, which are targeted at the needs of the elderly poor. It is unnecessary to make social security, the single most successful program, simultaneously promote all objectives of elderly assistance.

RATIONALE FOR SOCIAL SECURITY

Social security's role in financing the individual's elderly years is well established. In the program's four decades of operation there have been no major changes; policymakers have confined themselves to tinkering with benefit and payroll tax levels. Although transition to any other system would be both politically difficult and painful, it is still instructive to ask why a program such as social security would be instituted today. In conducting this assessment, one must be aware of the limitations of other institutional arrangements. For example, the welfare system is highly inefficient and poorly regarded. And to date the nation has had no success in implementing a negative income tax program.

The first motivation for assisting the elderly is that, as a group, the aged are poor, even with the help of income and in-kind transfers.[11] Although government transfer programs have eliminated abject poverty among the elderly, the number of near-poverty elderly is quite large.[12] Thus, 50.2 percent of married elderly have after-transfer incomes below $5,000; for single males and females the figures are 83.6 percent and 86.7 percent, respectively. By almost any standard, the elderly are the nation's most readily identifiable impoverished group. To illustrate, wherever one draws the poverty line between $3,000 and $5,000, there will be a greater proportion of the elderly below that line than of blacks of similar sex and marital status.

One reason why aid to the elderly is politically acceptable as well as desirable is that they are restricted—physically, through the market, and by government policy—in their ability to improve their own plight. Both in pre-elderly and elderly years, there are substantial barriers to providing for one's own old age.

Consider first an individual setting aside funds for his old age. The principal characteristic of this problem is uncertainty: he doesn't know how long he will live, what his other income sources will be, or what his medical needs will be. In short, he has highly imperfect information about an intrinsically probabilistic process. And, unlike most of his consumer choices, he has no opportunity for learning through trial and error.

When risks are important, insurance can play a useful role. Annuities, for example, if available on an actuarially fair basis, would be helpful in guarding against the risks of an uncertain life span. Without such a mechanism, an individual setting aside funds for his old age risks running out of funds if he "unfortunately" lives a long time; alternatively, if he dies early, he would be in the wasteful position of leaving an excessive estate. Unfortunately, because of large transactions costs and problems of adverse selection (those with long life expectancy would be most likely to join the insurance pool), private annuities are not available on an actuarially fair basis. Individuals saving privately for their own old age must strike a balance between saving too much if they die early or consuming too swiftly if they die late.[13] Uncertainties about expenditure needs (for example, housekeeper services, should minor disability occur), the ability to earn income, and returns on investment complicate their decision problem. A compulsory social insurance program such as social security can be justified as a response to imperfections in the markets for capital and in the type of insurance represented by annuities. Compulsion eliminates adverse selection and will likely reduce the costs of drawing contracts.

Social security plays a second role quite different from any insurance function. It offers what, in effect, is an attractive savings opportunity. This opportunity is important because of government policies that discourage savings and therefore any effort to provide for one's old age. Income from savings is taxed, of course, which means that individuals must invest at net rates that are well below effective rates of return on capital—the rates that would be available in a freely competitive system. In an inflationary period this problem is compounded, for both interest rates and capital gains in part reflect efforts to maintain real dollar values. Our tax system, unfortunately, is not structured to recognize that these inflation-compensating gains are not elements of income.

Pensions are a more effective means of providing for old age, particularly since they receive favorable tax treatment. However, only a small fraction of American workers have significant pension coverage. In 1968, for example, only 55 percent of all nonfarm employees were covered by any type of pension. For many, the amount of benefit rights earned so far is quite low (Beier 1971). The recently introduced Keogh plans and Individual Retirement Accounts offer many of the tax advantages of pension plans to individuals who are self-employed or whose employers have no pension program. Programs of this sort should be encouraged, since they enable individuals to provide for their own futures at close to market rates of return. At some far future date it is conceivable that the prevalence of these programs, together with fair annuities, will make self-provision for old age a potentially attractive alternative to social security. For now, it must be recognized that imperfections in insurance and capital markets and poorly chosen tax policies conspire to make self-provision unattractive.

Even with unhindered self-provision possible, there still might be justifications for compulsory savings. Individuals may selfishly fail to allocate substantial funds to promote their own future well-being. John Smith at 25 may consider himself quite different from—and not fully sympathetic to—John Smith at 65, as the activities of smokers and LSD imbibers make clear. Even if individuals are fully altruistic towards their future selves, there is some incentive for self-beggaring behavior. They may not save at all, or may fail to allow for unfavorable contingencies, in the expectation that society at large will always provide funds should their future conditions prove unattractive. Society, unable to bind itself not to provide such assistance, can protect itself only by requiring the individual to provide for himself.

Self-provision in old age itself is not a reliable alternative. There are many impediments to earning income. Technological advance is likely to have rendered obsolete many skills of the elderly. Where capabilities remain relevant, they are unlikely to be in the most productive, advanced industries. Widespread mandatory retirement rules eject many elderly from their former places of work, where they had developed skills and personal contacts specific to the enterprise. It may not be possible to find a job with a similar establishment, either because that firm has a similar mandatory retirement rule, or because a worker may lose pension benefits if he works for a competitor, or because institutional factors—such as the need to provide medical benefits—make it unattractive to hire older workers. Moreover, new employees often begin in entry-level positions that would not be comparable to an elderly individual's former job. Not only may the older worker's skills be irrelevant to the available job openings—a phenomenon in part due to technological change and advance—but the enterprise may be unwilling to make a hiring or training investment in a worker who is expected to depart sooner than a junior counterpart.

Ill health, though overemphasized in elderly employment analysis, also may impede the ability of the elderly to engage in work activities or more strenuous forms of work. Only a small percentage of the elderly give ill health or disability as a reason for being outside the labor force—16.4 percent for males 60 and over, and 8.5 percent for females 60 and over.[14]   The ill health or death of the principal family breadwinner may prompt elderly women to decide to enter the labor force, but if they have been unemployed for a long period their opportunities will be limited. Finally, many government programs for the elderly—social security and SSI in particular—impose substantial penalties on elderly earnings in terms of foregone benefits. We shall return to this problem in the next section.

As a group, then, the elderly are predominantly poor, in part because fair markets were not available to enable them to save and insure for their old age, but also because their present earning capabilities are limited and discouraged. The combination of these factors suggests that it is reasonable to consider transferring resources to individuals in the elderly population. Such aid has other attractive features. Unlike aid to most impoverished groups, assistance to the elderly is widely accepted, in part because of general recognition of the group's inability to help itself. Perhaps equally important, the elderly comprise a minority group we all can hope to join. Helping the elderly has a strong implicit contractual element, with future self-interest being the quid for the quo of present support. Because policymakers as a group tend to be both mature and affluent and can expect to join the elderly in disproportionate numbers, they have a strong personal stake in an assistance program like social security.

Assistance on an age-related basis also has strong theoretical appeal, since age is an immutable personal attribute. Unlike income-related assistance, no disincentives need arise from aid based on age. (Unfortunately, the present structure of social security penalizes the earnings of the elderly, partially subverting this advantage.) Finally, age is a readily monitorable variable that cannot easily be misrepresented. The government has at its disposal an array of personal information files, social security records in particular, which document an individual's age.

In short, a program of income support for the elderly has strong merits either on distributional grounds or to compensate for market imperfections and distortionary tax policies. In addition, income assistance based on age has political and economic advantages not shared by other forms of aid to disadvantaged groups.

THE COSTS OF SOCIAL SECURITY

In an earlier section, we detailed the principal benefits of social security in terms of providing a retirement income for the elderly. Because of the low administrative costs of the program (just over 1 percent of total benefits), the dollar values of benefit payments and of payroll taxes roughly cancel out. From society's standpoint, we would argue, the benefits from the transfer outweigh the payroll tax costs, both because of the redistributional gains derived from assisting the elderly poor and because of the market improvement made possible by instituting a compulsory annuity system. In particular, as already mentioned, the insurance benefits of social security will lead the elderly to value the benefits at more than their dollar cost.

An additional and less visible program cost is the inefficiency that the payroll tax causes by altering the work incentives of those contributing to the program. Although there is no empirical evidence that these disincentive effects are extensive, the significance of this aspect of program cost will increase as the payroll tax rate continues to rise and as working wives, now entering the labor force in large numbers, become better informed on how limited are the benefits that they receive in return for their payroll tax contributions.

Since the beginning of the program, its most widely discussed inefficiency has been that it forces individuals to save involuntarily. However, the low level of social security benefits and the continuance of individual saving despite strong discouragement weaken the argument that individuals would have chosen to allocate their funds very differently.

Disincentives for the Elderly Worker

The costs associated with the inefficiencies thus far discussed appear to be rather minimal. However, a final program cost—the discouragement of work by the elderly—is of particular concern for two reasons. First, the magnitude of the efficiency loss may be quite large. Second, the nature of the problem is critical to the welfare of the elderly. By inhibiting the elderly from working, social security deprives them of a principal means of financial support, partially undermining the income maintenance objective of the program.

The disincentive comes from the penalty on earnings of beneficiaries under age 72. Although the earnings penalty has been liberalized repeatedly, it remains harsh. After an elderly person's earnings reach $250 per month (in 1977), he foregoes 50 cents in social security benefits for each dollar earned. If he earns enough, he may lose his entire benefit. The penalty is incurred in addition to the usual deductions from earnings, such as payroll and federal income taxes. The net result is that the elderly may face marginal tax rates of 80 percent or more. Since the earnings test is removed for those 72 and over, this group does not suffer the 50 percent social security penalty. But those who have been outside the labor force (or working substantially reduced hours) for a prolonged period during the early portion of their elderly years will find reentry difficult.

The patterns of elderly labor force participation rates (LFPRs: the sum of the rates of employed and unemployed) reflect the influence of these kinds of forces. During the past century, for instance, a dramatic drop occurred in the percentage of elderly males and females in the labor force in the decade 1930-1940, when the social security program was instituted.[15] Elderly male LFPRs dropped from 73.9 percent of the elderly population in 1890 to 58.3 percent in 1930. The rate of decline accelerated during the next decade, with labor force participation dropping to 41.5 percent in 1940. By 1970 only one-fourth of all elderly males were in the labor force.

The female elderly have exhibited a very different pattern, with their LFPRs since 1890 fluctuating between 8 percent and 10 percent. As with their male counterparts, the largest drop (from 8 percent to 5.9 percent) occurred from 1930 to 1940. Though one might attribute this pattern to the generally depressed economic conditions of the 1930s, the changes were much starker for the elderly than for any other age group. Indeed, female LFPRs for those aged 25-64 rose significantly in that period. Although the richness of accompanying trends makes this historical evidence less than conclusive, it suggests the negative long-run impact that social security has had.

Our examination of more recent time series data on a monthly basis from 1966 to 1974 and on an annual basis from 1952 to 1971 yielded similar results. In particular, a strong negative relationship was evident between elderly LFPRs and the level of average social security benefits per recipient. For elderly males aged 65-69, a $100 increase in average benefits would be accompanied by a drop of 7.4 points in that group's rate of participation.[16] The older males are influenced less starkly, as a $100 benefit increase would lower the employment rates of males aged 70 and over by only 1.1 points (a small effect, which is not statistically significant at the 5 percent level). Removal of the earnings penalty for much of this latter group no doubt helped reduce the program's impact.

In addition, higher permissible earnings amounts under social security were found to have a somewhat weaker positive influence on the fraction of elderly in the labor force. Boskin (1977) reached similar conclusions regarding social security's impact on retirement, using data on individual retirement behavior of the elderly.

Social security's dramatic effect is seen by the LFPRs of the different age groups as shown in Figure 1. For both males and females there is a steady decline in participation as the age cohort becomes older. The sharp drop at age 65 is particularly interesting,

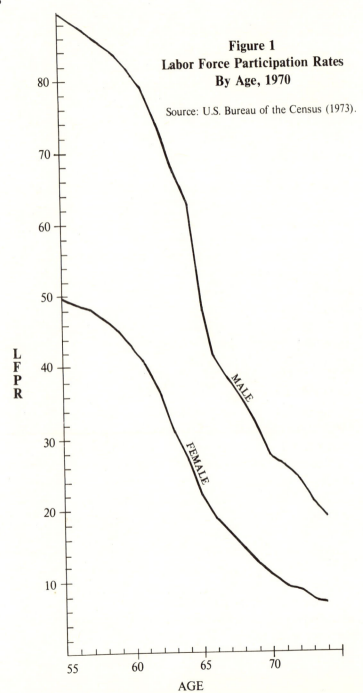

Figure 1
Labor Force Participation Rates
By Age, 1970

Source: U.S. Bureau of the Census (1973).

since that is when an individual can receive full social security benefits. Declining participation is less steep at age 72, when the earnings penalty is removed. The 1960 data we examined showed a more dramatic flattening of the relation between age and employment rates at age 72. The absence of a jump in LFPR at this age range reflects the difficulty of reentry into the labor force.

These results show that the primary impact of the earnings penalty is not to keep the few high earners off the benefit rolls, but to force a substantial portion of the elderly into retirement. Apart from its inefficiency, this impact also seems inequitable, since the elderly poor are hit hardest by the disincentives: they are poor in part because they respond to the disincentive. The professionals and managers, on the other hand, are able to earn enough above the penalty so that work may remain an attractive option. One cost of any transfer program results from the distortion of behavior to gain eligibility. Since this cost falls most heavily on the poor, including it in previously cited calculations for expected rates of return on contributions among different income groups would aggravate any disadvantage for the poor.

ELIMINATING THE EARNINGS TEST, AND OTHER TIMELY REFORMS FOR SOCIAL SECURITY

Removing the earnings test would clearly be desirable. It would permit the elderly to do more to help themselves, and would promote the efficient use of society's employment potential.

Three quite different arguments might be made in favor of an earnings test. First, it promotes a spreading of risk among the elderly. An individual who faces an uncontrollable event that may lead him to lose his work—perhaps a deterioration in physical condition—might prefer reduced benefits while he can work in order to buy protection when work is not possible. This argument would be compelling if most departures from the labor force were involuntary, or if the option of whether or not to retire were little influenced by the earnings test. But the evidence points in the opposite direction, particularly if we consider that the impact of the earnings test may extend to the employer's actions as well—say, when he formulates a retirement policy.

The second potential argument for an earnings penalty is that it removes the elderly from the work force, creating openings for younger workers. As traditionally posed, the argument is that society's unemployment rate can be reduced if the elderly are removed from the labor force; moreover, those remaining will be those who need work most. This line of reasoning is fallacious, however; in the long run, removing the elderly from the work force only reduces the scale of the economy, not the rate of unemployment. We would do as well to remove those whose names start with V and Z. A major unplanned experiment confirms our assertions. In the recent past, women have entered the labor force in unprecedented numbers; and while only preliminary analyses are available, no evidence suggests that this phenomenon will have more than a transitory effect on unemployment rates.

The third argument for an earnings test is that it improves the functioning of a labor market hindered by rigidities that prevent downward job mobility. Such mobility would be desirable if workers' skills obsolesce, or if their capabilities deteriorate with age. The structure of social security benefits, with the system's earnings test, establishes a target retirement age for the population. It relieves managers of the problem—particularly difficult, given likely worker or union opposition—of distinguishing which workers should be retired and which not. This is a rather crude use of the earnings test as a tool to improve labor market function. We have seen no evidence of its efficacy.

On balance, we believe these three arguments are weak, relative to those supporting removal of the earnings test. Our view is based in part on the increased need for society to allow—indeed encourage—the elderly to do more to help themselves.[17] Taxpayers are already complaining about the burdens imposed by assistance to the elderly, and the complaints would be far more bitter if the burden of the employer's tax share were correctly perceived.

Unfortunately, burdens on the work force to support the elderly will increase substantially in the medium range future, though imprecise demographic projections make estimates uncertain. To be concrete, assume that total future aid levels per elderly person remain the same as in FY 1973, the year for which the aid mix breakdown was given earlier. All projections will be cast in real 1972 dollars, enabling future inflation rates to be factored out of the calculations. Total aid to the elderly is calculated by multiplying the average aid per elderly person in FY 1973 by the total number of elderly for the year in question. The supporting working population is estimated by projecting population structure in conjunction with 1972 age-specific and sex-specific employment rates. Future increases in productivity and shifts in employment rates are not considered.

The aid burden by the year 2000, under these assumptions, will not change appreciably. Since the elderly population for that time is now alive—as are most future workers for that period—selecting the appropriate census projection has little influence on the results. Census Bureau (1972a) Series E assumes an average of 2.1 births per woman, close to the average for women aged 18-24 in 1972.[18] Given the projected population in the year 2000 with FY 1973 aid levels and 1972 employment rates, the aid burden would be $659— or only 1.003 times the 1972 burden. A lower birthrate has little influence on the calculations. Using Census Bureau (1972a) Series F, which assumes 1.8 average births per woman, yields a total aid burden per worker of $673, or only 1.025 times the 1972 cost.

The invariance of the aid burden from 1972 to 2000 is interesting but not surprising. In the year 2000 the percentage of elderly persons in society will decline, because of the entry of the low-birth, depression-era generation into old age. Those presently in their forties and older can look forward to fairly secure funding in old age.

Things are much bleaker for the individuals who are now in their twenties or thirties. During the decade 2010 to 2020, the aid burden will rise as members of the postwar baby boom enter old age. Projections for this period are particularly sensitive to assumed birthrate patterns. Employing Census Bureau (1972b) Series W (with immigration)—which is an intermediate projection that assumes a fertility rate of 2.11 births per woman—and assuming the FY 1973 aid level, the aid burden per worker would total $955 by the year 2025, or 1.454 times the 1972 level.

The actual burden, of course, could rise or fall from these levels depending on the pattern of future birth and death rates, LFPRs, and the productivity of different economic inputs. The proportional burden of elderly aid would be increased by any efforts that limit the growth of the economy. Uncertainty about the projections' accuracy should not lull us into ignoring their implications. The most likely outcome is that even current levels of aid will impose substantially greater burdens on future workers. When this happens, taxpayer resistance may force a reduction in per capita aid to the aged.[19]

Increasing the efficiency of existing aid might seem to offer a promising way to avoid increasing the tax burden. Suppose, for example, that all in-kind transfers other than Medicare, Medicaid, and VA aid programs were eliminated and that all of the funds were reallocated to pay social security benefits. The total amount gained by abolishing food stamps for the elderly, the Foster Grandparents Program, housing programs for the elderly, and all other efforts of this type would only save $3.42 billion in FY 1973, permitting cash grants to the elderly to be increased only 7.5 percent.

Redesigning the three sets of health programs might produce other economies. However, even eliminating the total amount allocated for in-kind aid, including Medicare, Medicaid, and VA aid programs—which would, of course, reduce elderly welfare—would still leave the 2015 aid burden 12.7 percent greater than in FY 1973. Even a substantial overestimate of possible economies does not eliminate the increase in costs to society of supporting its elderly population. The important lesson about in-kind aid to the elderly is negative. The present balance of cash and in-kind aid is not conspicuously out of line. However, the current tendency to move away from money assistance will be aggravated by political pressures to hold the line on the payroll tax for social security, and therefore policymakers should be vigilant in preventing any substantial shift towards in-kind programs and the strong potential inefficiencies they entail.

The solution to providing for the elderly is not merely to let the elderly get more from the expenditures we make for them but to encourage them to help themselves. Innovative policies should be considered. Opportunities certainly should be expanded for the pre-elderly to make untaxed allocations for their old age. The government might even subsidize such savings, assuming that social objectives would be served by increasing elderly as opposed to mid-aged consumption.

A major direction of reform should be to remove criteria for receiving elderly assistance. Removal of the earnings test for social security should be the first priority. Although benefit costs would increase as a result, sources of revenue do exist to finance the change. We would suggest that the income taxes of the working elderly be earmarked for social security, to preserve the program's image and the dignity of recipients.[20]

Second priorities would be removal of asset, residence, and marital status requirements. Even with demonstrated physical incapacity, home care may not be paid for in situations where substantially more expensive nursing-home care would be. Payments to a married couple of retirees are frequently below payments that the two would receive as single beneficiaries. Anecdotal evidence suggests that for financial purposes many widowed individuals may be "living in sin" while preferring remarriage, and the long-married may even be getting divorced for that reason. Restructuring programs to link benefits predominantly to age, to past contributions (where appropriate), and to medical condition would eliminate present incentives that discourage both self-help in old age and attempts to provide for retirement in prime earning years. Beyond the purely economic issues, weighing the full social and psychological costs of pushing the elderly into dependency make policies encouraging the elderly to help themselves substantially more attractive.

CONCLUSION

Four decades after its inception, social security remains the most important mechanism for supporting a predominantly disadvantaged group, the elderly. Over this period, however, the economic underpinning of the program has changed dramatically. Social security was enacted as one component of the attack on problems created by the Great Depression. Today it is justified as an effective response to the problems and discouragements of providing for one's own old age.

Unfortunately, by imposing a significant tax on elderly earnings, social security forces its beneficiaries into dependency. For too long we have treated the elderly as a burden to be borne by the rest of society. It is time to let the elderly make their contribution to society—and through past as well as present efforts, to their own welfare.

IV

DONALD O. PARSONS   **DOUGLAS R. MUNRO**

INTERGENERATIONAL TRANSFERS IN SOCIAL SECURITY

Ratio of benefits to taxes. Intergenerational transfer process. The welfare component of social security. Comparison of benefit cohorts. Ratio of retirees to workers.

INTRODUCTION

The current social security system is an odd mixture of old age insurance and welfare provisions. A number of practices suggest it is an insurance program, beyond the political rituals proclaiming it so. Benefits are at least loosely tied to contributions; generally, those with higher past incomes receive higher benefits. The benefits are unaffected by the recipient's physical wealth and asset income. The tax—or payments—are proportional to earnings up to a moderate level, then zero.

From a welfare program perspective, one might note the relatively tenuous relationship between benefits and contributions.

The benefits depend on characteristics under the control of the individual, particularly the presence of a spouse; and benefits are reduced by labor earnings beyond a fairly low threshold. A number of economists have suggested reforms which would either push the system towards an insurance format,[1] or alternatively, towards an income transfer or welfare program.[2] Whether the social security system should be developed more as a pure insurance program or more as a welfare program is a debatable issue. One's position toward it will largely reflect one's satisfaction with the current distribution of income. We argue below, however, that the current system is not uniform in its treatment of individuals *over time,* and as currently designed is fundamentally defective as a welfare instrument.

Welfare or unearned income transfers in the system are of two types: transfers within a given generation, and transfers between generations. Within a retirement cohort, benefits need not—and, in fact, are not—distributed proportionately to contributions or taxes paid. Welfare or transfers also occur between generations to the extent *average* benefits to a retirement cohort are higher than average contributions from that cohort would otherwise support.

Transfers within a retirement cohort are well recognized in public discussion. One crude measure of such redistribution is the ratio of monthly benefits to average taxable wages. Take a worker with thirty years' credit in the system and no spouse. Table 1 shows this benefit to wage base ratio for 1976. Although absolute levels of the ratios are not terribly instructive, the reduced ratio with higher taxable earnings is so. The worker who earned on average $100 per month (subject to social security taxes) over his work life receives almost $200 in monthly benefits when he retires. Because of the special minimum provision, an individual with twice the taxable earning ($200) only increases his benefits by 2 percent, or less than $5. Even beyond the special minimum, the benefits rise slowly with earnings taxed. The rise from $200 to $300, a 50 percent rise in taxable earnings (and implicitly in taxes paid), generates an increase in benefits only half as large (25 percent). Whether this degree of progressivity is felt to be an unfair burden on the diligent worker or heartlessly insensitive to the needs of the poor is largely

Table 1

The Ratio of Social Security Benefits to Taxable Wages for a Worker with Thirty Years' Credit, 1976

Average Monthly Taxable Wages[a]	Benefits	Benefits-Wages Ratio
$ 75	$180.90 [b]	2.41
100	180.90 [b]	1.81
150	180.90 [b]	1.21
200	185.20	.93
300	231.60	.77
400	279.80	.70
500	323.40	.65
600 [c]	371.50	.62

Source: Commerce Clearing House, Inc., "Social Security Benefits 1976" (Chicago, 1975).

[a] After dropping five lowest taxable earnings years.

[b] Special minimum for workers thirty years in the system.

[c] Maximum possible for retire in 1976.

a matter of opinion. The extent of wealth redistribution is clearly defined and the issue of progressivity subject to public scrutiny and debate.

Less well appreciated is the massive transfer which occurs between generations under the current system. The nature of this transfer process is poorly understood and the magnitude of the transfers largely unknown. It is this welfare aspect of the social security system which is our principal cause for concern and is the focus of this paper.

A retirement cohort may be said to have an intergenerational welfare—or simply welfare—component in its social security benefits if it receives more benefits than it could have earned from contributions and accrued interest. To anticipate the findings reported below, the welfare percentage of social security is high, but declining over time. The absolute size of the welfare component, however, has continued to grow, and rivals in size the sum of all other federal, state, and local public assistance programs.

A number of economists have argued that the tradition of each generation of workers transferring income to the generation too old to work is itself an "investment" process which, under ideal circumstances, may yield higher returns than are possible in the normal credit market.[3] But this is only true if total economic growth (growth in per capita income plus population) exceeds the market rate of interest. Unfortunately, this does not appear to be the case in the United States, where the rate of income growth has been substantially less than the rate of interest. It is not hard to grasp the general nature of the ideal conditions, or—more important—the consequences of operating such a system in a world of fluctuating conditions.

The intergenerational savings model shares many characteristics with the well-known "chain letter" scheme, though with a crucial difference. Under this system, working individuals transfer income to retired workers and receive in return assurance that they will receive even larger transfer income when they retire. A chain letter scheme must quickly collapse as the nearly instantaneous doubling and redoubling of transfers rapidly lead to transfers exceeding total resources. In the social security system, however, the process is extended over time; and when resource claims grow, the resource base required to support them may also grow. The social security structure, then, need not collapse either quickly or inevitably so long as the resource base grows with sufficient vigor and regularity. However, if the economic growth rate is lower than the rate of interest, this process is a poor "investment" for young workers. (See the discussion in Chapter V.)

If the system did collapse, however, the total consequence on the system would be identical to the collapse of the chain letter scheme. Neither creates new consumable resources, but rather reallocates existing resources. The gainers and losers in the playing of these games are determined by the date of entry into the game. Resources are transferrred from those entering just before the end of the chain to those lucky enough to have entered the chain earlier.

The gains and losses from either chain need not be great—many may receive modest profits or losses. Below we report estimates of the net welfare payments which have flowed to the retirement cohorts under the social security system from 1940 to 1970. As we shall see, the fortunate circumstances of early entrants cannot be extended into the future.

SOCIAL SECURITY AS AN INTERGENERATIONAL WEALTH TRANSFER PROCESS

Before presenting the historical evidence on past and current levels of intergenerational transfers, we should explain more carefully how the system operates as a transfer device. The welfare component of social security ideally should be determined by the desire of current workers to help older and presumably poorer individuals. In fact, the welfare component in the present system seems to be determined largely by the independent decisions of its component elements—the average benefit level and the tax revenue constraints. Below we examine patterns in the decisions about benefit and tax levels—which combine to produce the welfare component.

The Behavior of Benefits

Benefit payments under social security have followed a pattern similar to other welfare payments, particularly since 1950. Average monthly benefits for a worker and spouse have risen from about $68 per month in 1950 to $178 per month in 1970. Average benefits for a family in the Aid to Families with Dependent Children program have risen from $72 per month to $187 per month over the same period. Figure 1 shows the similarity of payments over the period. Clearly the two series are closely related, although social

Figure 1

Annual Benefits, Social Security of Worker and Spouse and "Aid to Families with Dependent Children" Families

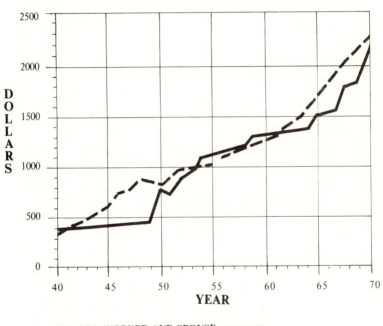

SOC. SEC. WORKER AND SPOUSE ▬▬▬

AFDC FAMILIES ▬ ▬ ▪

Source: *Historical Statistics of the United States, Colonial Times to 1970* (Washington, D.C., 1975).

security benefits have not been as steady over time, with sharp upward adjustments followed by periods of few benefit changes. Otherwise the series are quite comparable, which suggests that average benefit levels for the two groups results from the same collective preferences. Apparently the worker and nonworking spouse with no assets or pension other than social security receives on average the same income as the couple on welfare. Since higher earning workers receive higher retirement benefits, average social security benefit levels overstate the average benefits paid workers with no assets or other pensions. The main point here, however, is that benefits have followed a pattern comparable to other, unrelated programs—which suggests that benefit levels are set by some common notion of a minimal decent level of income.

Benefit levels for social security and the AFDC program have risen in rough proportion to average personal income per capita (see Figure 2). Since 1950 average social security benefits for a retired worker and spouse have remained fairly constant at 50-60 percent of U.S. personal income per capita. The minimal acceptable level of support indicated by these two programs apparently is a regular fraction of personal income.

The Behavior of Taxes

Since the program's inception, tax levels have followed a similar pattern. A self-financing system that minimizes taxes while maximizing the welfare component is one which equates current taxes and benefits. Such a pay-as-you-go system has been a hallmark of social security almost from the beginning . Figure 3 shows the flow of expenditures (benefits) and tax revenues (contributions) from 1940 to 1970. The system has clearly followed a pattern of collecting enough taxes to pay current benefits.

The Welfare Component

If benefits are set by some criterion of a minimal acceptable standard of living related to current national income, and if taxes are set by the criterion that current taxes must equal current expen-

Figure 2

**Annual Social Security Benefits of Retired Worker and
Spouse as a Fraction of United States
Personal Income per Capita**

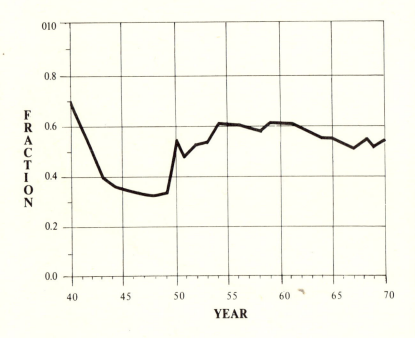

Source: *Historical Statistics.*

Figure 3

**Annual Social Security Contributions and Benefits
(in millions of dollars), 1940-1970**

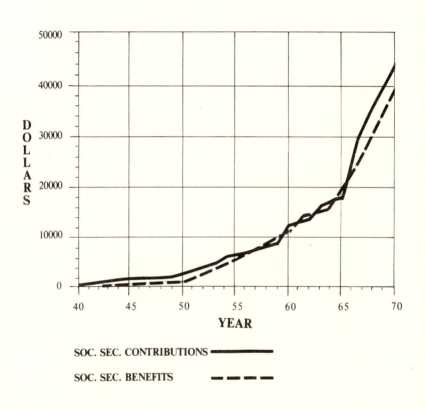

Source: *Historical Statistics.*

ditures, than the welfare fraction of social security is a residual. The system will work best for a given generation of retirees if the economy is large and growing. Two components are particularly important—the growth rate in per capita income and the ratio of retirees to workers.

Lowering the proportion of retirees to workers reduces the tax load each worker must bear to support a given level of benefits per retiree, and therefore implies a higher future welfare ratio. Increasing economic growth benefits the welfare ratio, since average future benefits rise with national income while past taxes would have been lower. Since tax payments increase with time in the system while benefits do not, greater maturity of the system inevitably reduces the welfare ratio.

THE WELFARE COMPONENT OF SOCIAL SECURITY: THE HISTORICAL RECORD, 1940-1970[4]

In estimating the welfare component of social security, estimated contributions plus interest (at private market rates) are compared to the discounted value of expected benefits for each retirement cohort. Alternatively, the procedure can be described in annual terms by comparing social security benefit levels with a hypothetical lifetime annuity that could be purchased in the private market with the same contributions plus interest. An example will illustrate the form of the calculations undertaken, and will provide historical insight into the reasons why the system began operating on a "pay-as-you-go" rather than a fully funded basis.

An Example: The First Benefit Cohort

The social security program first began collecting taxes in 1937, with benefits first distributed in 1940. Consider, then, the welfare component for an individual who was 62 in 1937 and retired in 1940 at 65, assuming that the worker earned more than the maximum taxable base earnings of $3,000 so that he made the maximum contribution. Both the employee and the employer paid 1 percent of the maximum tax base of $3,000, so each contributed

$30 per year, or a combined annual total of $60. Assuming the individual saved $60 per year and it paid 6 percent interest (double the rate prevalent at the time), after three years he would have accumulated $202.48 from which to draw benefits. Given the average life expectancy of a person age 65 in 1940, a private annuity program would pay him $25.67 *per year,* or about $2 per month. Such a plan would have had little economic interest for the retiree.

These calculations, it should be stressed, generate *maximum* earned benefits. The average worker would have earned substantially less, since average earnings were less than $3,000 and interest rates less than 6 percent. For a worker making average earnings and investing at interest rates then prevailing, the retirement sum in 1940 would be only $68.36, yielding an annuity of $6.59 per year. Clearly benefits far in excess of contributions would be required if any substantial benefits were to be paid.

The actual average annual benefit paid in 1940 to a male age 65 was $270.60. Since an annuity would yield only $6.59, $264.01 of the benefits are a pure transfer, or welfare payment. Since the benefits may—and, in fact, did—change over the retirement period, it is more convenient to compare capitalized savings and benefits over the expected time span than to compare annuity payments and annual benefits. If the tax and benefit payments are known for each year of expected life (accounting for any legislative increases), and discounted to the date of retirement using the interest rate prevailing at the date of retirement, we may calculate the present value of the lifetime welfare payment. For the individual in question, the present value of lifetime benefits is $2,962.09, of which $2,893.73 is a transfer. In other words, this individual paid for only 2.3 percent of the benefits he received.

The Results

For each retirement cohort a similar calculation was made of the present value of average cohort tax payments and benefits at the age of retirement.[5] The calculations differ for different individuals in a given age cohort, depending on their expected retirement age and mortality record. Here we report the time trends of the welfare

Figure 4

Social Security as Implicit Welfare, Fraction of Total Benefits by Annual Retirement Cohorts, 1940-1970*

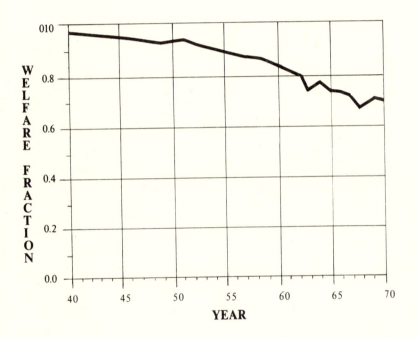

Source: Douglas R. Munro, "Welfare Component and Labor Supply Effects of
         OASDHI Retirement Benefits" (Ph.D. dissertation, Ohio State
         University, 1976).
*Male, age 65 retirees.

Figure 5

The Ratio of Capitalized Social Benefits to Contributions by Annual Retirement Cohorts, 1940-1970*

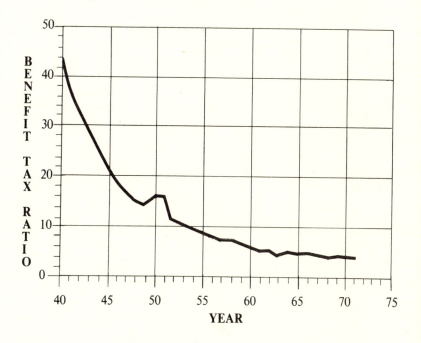

Source: Munro, *op. cit.*
*Male, age 65 retirees.

component for males who retire at age 65, the largest group of retirees. The welfare ratio for females is somewhat higher, and the ratio for males who postpone retirement beyond 65 somewhat lower. But the general form of the time relationship is much the same for all groups.[6]

Figure 4 shows the ratio of the welfare component of benefits to total benefits for cohorts of age 65 retirees from 1940 to 1970. The same relationship is shown in Figure 5 in terms of the ratio of benefits to contributions. The welfare fraction has declined sharply over the period, from about 98 percent in 1940 to 68 percent in 1970. The fraction for similar females has declined from 99 percent to 80 percent over the same period . The ratio for females receiving benefits on their own records is higher, because social security benefits are progressive (higher earnings are awarded proportionately less benefits), and female earnings on average are less. If unearned spouse benefits were included, the welfare percentage would be higher still, since unearned spouse benefits are about one-third the size of primary benefits.

While the welfare ratio of an individual's benefits has declined over the period, the absolute level of welfare payments per recipient has been steadily increasing—so much so that the increasing size of total benefits has more than offset the declining ratio of welfare to total benefits. The trend in individual present values of welfare for cohorts of male, age 65, retirees is presented in Figure 6. In 1970 it had reached a level of about $16,000 per retiree.

The Future

How has the system managed to pay off its participants at such a generous rate, not only during the early years but continuously up to 1970, thirty years later? The answer to this question sheds light on the question of the system's future.

Three factors play a role. The most obvious is the start-up phenomenon. The longest a 1970 retiree could have been covered by social security is thirty-three years. Workers in the future who work consistently throughout can expect to work forty to forty-five years before receiving benefits. They then will have worked and

Figure 6

The Present Value of the Welfare Component of Social Security Benefits per Retiree, Retirement Cohorts, 1940-1970*

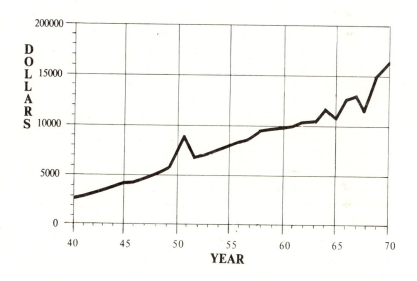

Source: Munro, "Welfare Component and Labor Supply Effects."
*Male, age 65 retiree.

paid social security payroll taxes over approximately one-third more years. Assuming benefits continue to be gauged by independent factors (such as some minimum decent living standard), the tax/benefit ratio will rise by one-third as well—which adjustment, by itself, would lower the 1970 welfare ratio from 70 percent to 60 percent.

Two other forces were at work to drive up the welfare ratio. Over most of the period, economic growth per capita has been substantial, increasing the resource base from which retirees are supported. During the period 1940-1970, real gross national product per capita grew on average 2.4 percent per year.

A much more important factor has been the ratio of retirees to workers. The tax rate per worker depends on the number of retirees a worker must support over his work life. Because the system was starting up, the ratio of retirees to workers has been quite low over much of the work life of 1970 retirees. Table 2 shows for five-year intervals the ratio of retirees to workers covered by social security over the period 1940-1970. The ratio rises from less than one in one hundred to almost twenty in one hundred. Thus, over their work lives, individual workers retiring in 1970 supported retirees at a rate of less than one retiree for every ten workers. If 1970 retiree-to-worker ratios had persisted throughout the thirty-year period, total taxes paid would have doubled, as would the tax-to-benefits ratio. Eliminating the two separate start-up effects—the short interval of tax payments for some workers, plus the unusually high ratio of workers to retirees—would have reduced the 1970 welfare ratio from about 70 percent to 20 percent.

Needless to say, the retiree-to-worker ratio is a crucial factor, and unfortunately it is likely to rise further in the foreseeable future because of unfavorable demographic trends. The future ratio of retirees to workers will depend on a variety of factors including retirement age, labor force participation, etc. The fundamental underlying factor, however, is the age profile of the population. If the ratio of old to young rises, the retiree-to-worker ratio will also likely rise. Figure 7 illustrates the current age profile of the male population, and makes clear why past demographic trends have been

Table 2

The Ratio of Retirees to Covered Employment, 1940-1970

Year	Ratio
1970	.185
1965	.169
1960	.119
1955	.081
1950	.045
1945	.012
1940	.004
Average	.088

Source: *Historical Statistics,* p. 348.

favorable to the system as well as why future trends may not be.

The profile reflects a wide range of demographic experiences over the last fifty years. The low fertility of the depression years followed by the postwar baby boom are both apparent in the profile. The most bothersome trend, however, from the system's viewpoint, is the recent decline in births. If it continues, this trend will have a serious impact on the value of the system for retirees.

The retiree/worker ratio will probably grow over the next fifty years, even if current trends in birthrates are reversed. Table 3 shows the ratio of males 65 and over to those in the prime working years (21-64) under three different fertility assumptions—2.7, 2.1, and 1.7 (average number of births per woman). Current averages have been slightly under 2.0.

Figure 7

The Age Distribution of Males in the U.S. in
Five Year Age Intervals, 1975

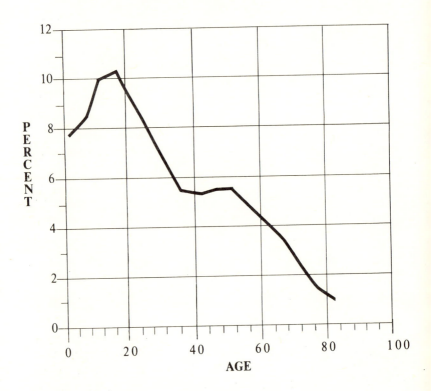

Source: U.S. Bureau of the Census, Current Population reports, Series P-25, No.
601, 1975.

Table 3

Ratio of Males 65 and Older to Males 21-64 for Selected Years, 1975-2050

Year	Average Births per Woman		
	2.7	2.1	1.7
1975	.167	.167	.167
2000	.163	.165	.167
2025	.203	.242	.278
2050	.178	.237	.297

Source: U.S. Bureau of the Census, *Current Population Surveys,* Series P-25, no. 601.

The ratio in 1967 is .167, and apparently will remain unchanged over the next twenty-five years. By the year 2025, however, the ratio will rise by 20 percent even under the highest fertility rate assumption; by 45 percent under a moderate rate; and by 66 percent under the lowest—but still quite possible—assumption of something less than two children per woman. By 2050, if birthrates remain at the level of 1.7 per woman, the retiree ratio will almost double from current levels. Each retiree would be supported by 3.33 workers.

If even the middle fertility assumption is accurate in the long run, the 50 percent rise in the retiree ratio will have important consequences, inducing a 50 percent rise in the real burden of the system; and in a mature system this would be without any start-up profits. It is quite likely that even under favorable income growth assumptions, workers retiring in the next generation will find that the social security system is quite unfavorable to them.

CONCLUSION

The current social security system has been a profitable venture for workers in past and even current cohorts. For a single male retiring in 1940 at age 65 after three years in the system, fully 98 percent of his benefits were unearned. For a single male retiring in 1970 at age 65 after thirty-three years in the system, a substantial 68 percent of his benefits were (are) unearned. The welfare component for a married man of 65 with nonworking spouse (over age 62) is higher, since such men qualify for additional benefits (about 50 percent) without additional tax liabilities.

The good fortune of early participants in the system is not a useful measure of the returns to all generations, since a number of start-up factors affect even the 1970 retirement cohort. They have been in the system and paid significantly lower taxes than will later generations—and they have been required to support substantially fewer retirees during the years they were in the system. The future trend in the ratio of retirees to workers suggests that the system will become substantiallly more burdensome over the next fifty years, since birthrates—and therefore the supply of future workers—have dropped sharply. With the disappearance of start-up advantages over the same period, the future of the system does not seem happy.

The current dimension of the intergenerational welfare payments is sobering: it rivals in magnitude the total of all other government public assistance programs. A crude measurement of the annual welfare component of social security retirement benefits—calculated by multiplying benefits paid workers in a given year times the welfare ratio for the retiree cohort in that year plus spouse benefits—reveals aggregate annual welfare payments under social security of almost $16 billion in 1970. In the same year, total public assistance programs, including transfers in kind such as food stamps, dispersed $16.5 billion. The trends in the two series over the period 1940-1970 appear in Figure 8.

In fifty years these intergenerational transfers will likely disappear and may in fact become negative, even if the system continues to operate. The question immediately arises whether it is desirable

Figure 8

Annual Implicit Social Security Welfare and Annual Total Public Assistance (in millions of dollars) 1940-1970*

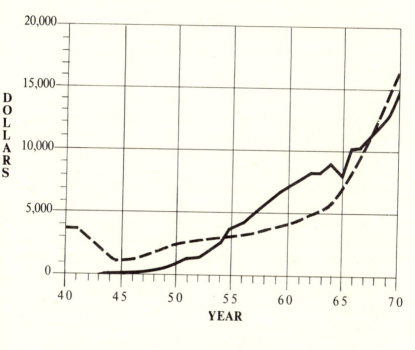

Source: *History Statistics;* Munro, "Welfare Component and Labor Supply Effects."

*Social Security retirement programs only.

that a system dole out huge windfalls to one generation and huge losses to another, purely on vagaries in the birthrate. In retrospect, it would have been prudent to have taxed more heavily in the early years to provide a fund to cushion at least modest variations in birthrates and thereby treat generations more evenly. Only a fully funded system would have protected each generation from adverse demographic shifts.

The current system, however, is not one we can easily eliminate. Once huge transfers have been made in the first generations, no generation has an incentive to stop. For the last generation to pay into the system must then bear the cost of repaying the generous treatment of *all* past generations. Instead of losing some fraction of their investment in the system, they will lose it all.

This last problem lives, however, in the shadow of a giant potential counterforce. While no generation wants to stop, the incentives are not the same for all workers in a generation. Those nearing retirement, who have paid in longest, have greatest incentive to continue; the youngest, however, who have paid in little, have much less to lose by withdrawing. The younger they are, therefore, the more likely it is that they may calculate their dilemma and press politically to withdraw. These strikingly divergent interests may create dangerous political and social tensions—as well as affect behavior in ways that are extremely difficult to predict. The longer policymakers delay in addressing the long-term problem, the more serious it will become. The "long term" usually refers to the moment direct economic consequences are felt. The *real* problem, however, will come long before that, as increasing numbers reflect their future expectations in their current behavior. Growing public awareness of the problem could bring it all to crisis considerably before the long term happens.

V

SHERWIN ROSEN

SOCIAL SECURITY AND THE ECONOMY

Retirement income sources. Intergenerational transfers. Social security and private security. Unfunded government debt and budget deficits. International comparisons of social security systems. Work income test and social security. Intragenerational income and tax distribution.

INTRODUCTION

This paper will review some of the intellectual debate and empirical evidence on the effects of social security on the general economy. Specifically, I shall consider distributional effects, as well as consequences for the supply of labor, and incentives for private capital accumulation.

The origins of social security and other social insurance programs in the U.S. go back to the severe economic disruptions of the 1930s, when the breakdown of social institutions revealed much about the limitations of private insurance markets. Yet those beginnings tend to mask the fact that social insurance does not proceed from a vacuum, but in part replaces and is offset by substitute arrangements within families that would otherwise take place. For this reason, social security and other social insurance programs must be analyzed in the context of the entire transfer economy, including the sector organized outside government auspices, especially in relation to the family.

The fundamental economic analysis of social security began with Samuelson's demonstration of how a system of intergenerational transfers can yield positive returns on each generation's tax payments when they are sustained by growth in population and productivity.[1] From the beginning, social security has stressed the twin goals of social adequacy and individual equity, the two natural foci of the fundamental paradox of social security. On the one hand, the program is an intergenerational tax-transfer scheme, under pay-as-you-go financing, which transfers resources from workers to retirees. On the other hand, it resembles an annuity system, since retirement benefits are linked more or less directly to one's "contributions" or taxes paid during working life. The fundamental difference betweeen such a system and private pensions and annuities lies in the financial reserve to the obligations incurred: private pension funds accumulate real physical capital, while social security pensions rest on taxing power.

For most persons, earnings are the chief source of income during working life, and they represent the returns on personal investments in schooling and other skill-augmenting activities that have value in the labor market. Lifetime earnings patterns are related systematically to age and to labor market experience. Earnings tend to rise rapidly in the first two decades of work life; growth slows during middle age, and slows more or even actually declines in the years just prior to retirement. The operations of financial markets and private savings decisions indicate that consumption patterns need not be directly geared to current income. Rather, they may be smoothed over the life cycle by abstaining from consumption when income is larger than normal, thus acquiring assets that have future productivity, and selling title to these assets and consuming the proceeds in periods when current income is below

Figure 1

A Typical Life-Cycle Pattern
of Income, Consumption and Saving

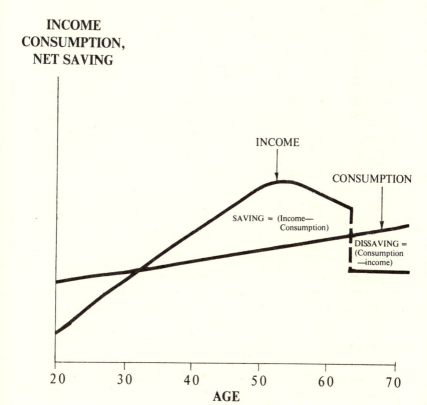

normal. While life cycle patterns of saving (and dissaving) follow systematic empirical patterns, the primary pattern we are concerned about is the net acquisition of assets during working years for use in years of retirement. Figure 1 depicts the pattern graphicallly. Of course, not all such asset accumulations need occur, and in fact all do not occur in financial markets. In part they are represented by investments in owner-occupied housing, durable goods, and so forth, whose very services provide implicit income (in kind). Whatever these distinctions turn out to be, the net saving undertaken during working life releases resources from consumption to investment in physical or human capital assets. After going through the intermediaries in the capital markets, the financial claims are titles to real capital that are valued in terms of their marginal contribution to output in the economy. In a growing economy net additions to the capital stock also occur within generations by inheritance.

ANALYTICAL FRAMEWORK

To illustrate the basic point, consider a simple example in which the economy has reached a steady state with a constant resource base and therefore constant output capacity. Gross saving in any year is just sufficient to maintain the capital stock; population is constant; and there is no productivity advance. In this setting we can envision two periods within each generation, working years and retirement years, and a series of two overlapping generations alive at any one time. The younger generation works; the older generation is retired. In this case the process described above becomes very simple: anticipating their retirement, young persons acquire title to the unchanged stock of capital at the rate at which their income exceeds their consumption. Members of the older generation, having acquired similar ownership rights in the preceding period, supply these claims and sell them for money to be spent on consumption goods released by the net saving of the young. The financial market equalizes saving by the young and dissaving by the old through a rate of interest that induces the young to abstain from consumption and acquire title to capital at exactly the same rate at which retirees desire to sell it off. And the process continues indefinitely. Thus, even without social insurance, forces exist to make the ownership of capital systematically revolve among successive overlapping generations. In addition to transfers through the market, direct gifts and bequests also play a role.

For many reasons a purely private and voluntary system of intergenerational transfers through the market and intrafamily bequests has not been considered adequate to meet society's needs. Most persons in society are unwilling to ignore random events that may harm some members or ignore the plight of improvident individuals or those who made bad investments. Some persons must throw themselves at the mercy of the state, and therefore it is appropriate to mandate pension enrollment during working years to provide some minimum level of support during retirement. Adverse selection makes a purely voluntary system unreliable.

At its inception, the U.S. social security system was seen as an insurance program mandating basic protection and support, and was based on reserve funding principles not unlike those used by private institutions (though with a portfolio devoted to government debt rather than private assets). In the early years when the number of eligible retirees was small in relation to the tax base, substantial surpluses and a considerable fund were accumulated. Finding it impractical and unnecessary to build up a full reserve fund, the system gradually converted to a pay-as-you-go method of finance. The early similarity with mandatory private pensions thus ended, although workers do accumulate credits loosely related to prior taxes. The current practice of more or less directly paying out tax receipts to retirees means that social security obligations have no counterpart in real physical capital in the economy. Social security taxes credited to individual accounts accumulate unfunded, implicit debt,[2] and the financial integrity of the system rests, as with all government debt, on the government's power to tax future working populations to pay benefits. While this method of financing would not be sound financial and actuarial practice for private pension plans, the same need not be true of the government because of its power to tax and because of its longer time horizon.

Many observers have appropriately compared social security's pay-as-you-go system with a chain letter;[3] but the analogy is not quite complete. Chain letters are unstable because they must end ultimately, which is not true of a pay-as-you-go intergenerational transfer.

A simple example will clarify the problem and highlight the essential nature of social security. Think of a situation in which population grows at a constant rate (for example, 1 percent per year) and there is no productivity advance. Under these circumstances national income will also grow at 1 percent per year, per capita income is constant, and total income merely expands at the rate at which new resources (additional labor) are added to the economy. To simplify, think of two overlapping generations alive during any period, as before, with the younger generation working and the older generation retired. The constant force of population growth means that more persons are born in successive generations, and the number of workers always exceeds the number of retirees. In this situation the ratio of retirees to workers in each period depends on the rate of population growth and the retirement age. If population doubled in each generation and each person spent half his life working and half retired (ignoring childhood), there would be twice as many workers as retirees. If population growth were 50 instead of 100 percent, there would be 50 percent more workers than retirees.

Now let the government impose a flat percentage wage tax on workers and immediately pay it all out to retirees in equal shares. Each retiree obviously receives more than the per capita tax payments because there are more workers than retirees. Put differently, each person as a retiree receives more transfer payments than the taxes he paid in the previous period, because the taxable base (the number of workers available times the output each one produces) is continually growing. For all generations except the first one, the ratio between the transfers received while retired and the taxes paid while working can be thought of as a "rate of return on investment" of an individual's social security contributions. The rate of return is much larger than this for the initial generation, because they are never taxed while young but nevertheless receive what amounts to a pure gift at the time the program is adopted. In one sense this gift is paid by the second generation; but there is a deeper sense in which it is not, because the second generation and succeeding generations pass the burden on successively from generation to generation. The burden is finally fully shifted to the last generation, who must pay a per capita tax but who receive nothing in return because there is no young generation left for them to tax. Evidently, if there is no "last" generation, if the economy has an indefinitely long lifetime, the burden of the gift to the initial generation is postponed forever. This is the sense in which the sytem's financial integrity depends on the power of the older generations to tax the younger.[4]

It is apparent, finally, that this implicit rate of return on prior tax payments is sustained by a growing taxable base, whatever its source. In the example above, the tax base grew because population was growing. However, the tax base also grows because there is a productivity advance manifest in increasing wage rates and higher standards of living. Thus essentially the same picture would emerge without population growth but with an equivalent growth of the real wage rate. If both population and the real wage rate grow, the implicit rate of return on social security taxes is correspondingly increased to equal approximately the sum of the two growth rates.

SOCIAL SECURITY AND PRIVATE SAVINGS

As discussed above, social security had no behavioral consequences on consumption-savings or employment decisions, so that real economic growth and output were independent of transfers. Yet most economic analysis suggests some kinds of behavior are affected by the government programs. That is no exception here.[5]

Return for a moment to the simple stationary economy in which titles to capital assets were transferred through the market from the old to the young at prices sufficient to induce the population to maintain the existing capital stock intact. Now introduce a social security system of the type described above and consider a representative person's behavior. The decision to save transfers purchasing power from working years to retirement years, when withdrawal from the labor force occurs and income from work ceases. The value of accumulating assets while young is proportional to the value of future income embodied in them. But from an individual's point of view, claims to real private capital are no different than social security credits accumulated through the payroll tax, since those credits also promise future income. Therefore social security credits representing implicit, unfunded debt have the same value for transferring income to retirement years as do claims to real assets. From a personal point of view, the two are perfect substitutes for each other. Thus one might expect social security pension claims to substitute dollar for dollar with other assets in private portfolios. Workers might as well consider their tax contributions as a form of personal savings, reducing the need to accumulate private assets. The result must reduce the demand for private assets backed by real capital.

Reduced demand for claims to physical assets has important real consequences for the economy and its productive capacity. Since the young are less willing to accumulate titles to private capital than before, the prices at which these assets will be willingly held must fall. Those who were previously dissaving must suffer capital losses when the system is introduced, partially offsetting their gift from social security. The more important effect, however, relates to the growth of capital in the economy. The declining price of capital assets means that producers find it less profitable to produce capital goods. Gross investment falls, and the capital stock must fall and be maintained at a lower level commensurate with its lower price. When the capital stock declines, less real resources are available to the economy and its total productive capacity has declined also. Per capita output falls and so does the real wage rate as labor becomes more abundant relative to capital. In a growing economy similar considerations apply, though the analysis is more complicated. In that case the economy would experience reduced per capita income after all adjustments have worked themselves out, with the same growth rate as before. There would also be a transition phase during which the growth rate of income and capital stock is less than it otherwise would have been, surely an important and heretofore unrecognized consequence of unfunded government pension systems. Notice that it is not the mandatory provisions of social security that are crucial here, since the govenment can mandate participation in private pension systems. Rather, *it is the substitution of unfunded government debt for real assets* that is the crux of the matter. Since the present unfunded liability of social security is on the order of four trillion dollars, this is a force that must be reckoned with.

There are two important potential offsets to this asset substitution effect. First is the effect of the social security earnings test on employment decisions of the elderly. Some of the evidence reviewed below suggests that the work retirement test will be likely to reduce the retirement age and constrain employment by older workers, thereby reducing the value of investments in one's earning power as a source of support during retirement and lengthening the period of retirement. A natural result is to increase the demand for private assets in working years to sustain living standards during a longer retirement period. It is often argued that the work retirement test stimulates incentives for thrift for this reason. There is a second, more subtle, and far-reaching possibility that government-provided pensions through social security may merely socialize many private intergenerational transfers that otherwise would have occurred.[6]

PRIVATE INTERGENERATIONAL TRANSFERS

The possibility that social security in part socializes private obligations deserves greater attention than it has received. It depends on the concept of an extended family spanning two or three generations, including children, workers, and retirees, and views the family as providing mutual insurance and self-protective functions similar to old-fashioned discussions of the family role. This view is very different from the summary analysis above, which implicitly considered each generation's decisions as independent of all other generations. This latter view is too simple. It is not adequate in a family context, because the very essence of families implies the sharing of resources and systematic intergenerational transfers among members outside the market mechanism. Ever since the decline of child labor and probably long before, substantial resources are transferred from parents to their children in the form of increasing education, health care, food consumption, and so forth, most of which improve the productivity of labor in successive generations. These expenditures seldom appear in the national accounts as acts of saving and investment in human agents of production, but they are significant elements of capital accumulation in the economy.[7] In considering the effects of social security on private capital formation, we must evaluate the program's effects on this type of capital as well as on physical capital.

The offset to the asset substitution effect that comes from private intergenerational transfers depends on whether children on balance support their parents over the life cycle, or vice versa. There is an offset either way. If parents transfer net wealth to their children, then increased social security benefits for retirees financed by payroll taxes on workers are at once a windfall to parents and a liability to their children. The increased wealth of retirees is counterbalanced exactly by the reduced wealth of their offspring because of the greater future tax liabilities necessary to finance greater benefits. If for simplicity we suppose that parents' bequests are set to ensure a fixed target claim to real resources, unanticipated benefits have the effect of increasing net bequests to heirs exactly by the amount of increased tax liability imposed on them. Or retirees can save the additional benefits, invest them at interest, and bequeath the accumulated proceeds to their heirs. Though the net indebtedness of offspring has increased, their total bequests have increased by more or less the same amount. These private transfers "undo" the social mandatory transfers. Of course, the different tax treatment of financial bequests and social security income may prevent completely offsetting effects, but one might imagine bequests as investments in kind (e.g., for education) rather than as outright claims to physical capital. Even so, any such forces must be tempered by limitations of family size and the extent of childless families. Also, many retirees report that social security benefits are their sole source of money income.

A more interesting situation may arise when net transfers go from children to parents, in the form of partial support during retirement years. If social security merely socialized transfers from workers to their parents, one would expect that the system's increasing maturity would reduce private support virtually dollar for dollar with mandated benefit levels. The government simply serves as an intermediary, with transfers channelled to the elderly through social security, rather than directly through the extended family. By instituting a claim by older generations on the fruits of their children's income-producing power in a dignified manner and as a matter of earned right, it is easy to see how this socialization might raise economic welfare by promoting independent household formation, reduced family strife, and so forth. This is undoubtedly a major reason for its widespread public support. So far as the effects on private capital accumulation are concerned, the offset works only against an initial source of family support. Also, while no one would argue that social security has been a factor in the breakup of the family, the direction of causality may well run in the opposite direction. Social security programs may be substituting for weakening family ties over time, in which case the force of the presumed offset of social security transfers replacing private obligations also may be weakening over time.

EMPIRICAL EVIDENCE

Recent research of this important question has focused on three independent sets of evidence. The first and most widely quoted has been time-series investigations of aggregate consumption and savings behavior over the 1929-1975 period. The second are international comparisons of social security systems in the developed world; and the third are cross-section studies of individual behavior.

The time-series studies have related per capita aggregate consumption to per capita income and wealth. They are distinguished from earlier studies of consumption and savings behavior by explicitly examining the effects of implicit social security wealth and labor force participation of the aged. Social security wealth is measured by outstanding obligations of the system to future retirees. Extrapolations for future changes in real benefit levels are based on prior experience, including major changes in coverage which, while important in the past, will be less so in the future because most workers are now covered. This variable is meant to represent the asset substitution effect analyzed above. Including measures of labor force participation by the aged captures the effects of the retirement offset. Unfortunately, no adequate measures of intrafamily private intergenerational transfers exist; they have not, therefore, been included in any of the studies and cannot be measured. Even so, the results of feasible studies are ambiguous and admit alternate interpretations. For example, Alicia Munnell has found that greater labor force participation by the aged increases aggregate consumption,[8] which is evidence for the retirement offset. But it may also reflect the fact that some of the elderly have chosen to invest more in human capital and earning power than in physical capital. It may also be true that the elderly who work have different attitudes toward thrift or different consumption wants than those who do not work. So far as the effects of social security wealth itself are concerned, two studies (by Martin Feldstein and Alicia Munnell) report negative effects on private savings.[9] Yet these results are not robust to alternate empirical specification, since social security wealth is highly correlated with other variables and may reflect these other effects rather than the asset substitution effect. For example, aggregate social security wealth relates closely to the unemployment rate in the pre-World War II period. It is therefore difficult to disengage the separate effects on savings of social security wealth and of transitory variations of income reflected in the unemployment rate.[10] Furthermore, in the postwar period social security wealth behaves much like a trend, and trendlike variables are always difficult to interpret. In this case they may be compounding other secular changes in family structure, such as the increased labor force participation of married women.

There have been several studies of institutional differences in social security systems among different countries, but only one thorough analytical study (by Feldstein) of their effects on savings and labor force participation.[11] International differences in benefit levels relative to income do seem to be associated with reduced private capital accumulation and lower rates of elderly labor force participation. However, the study was restricted to differences among developed countries for which the best data are available. Thus the range of observations is restricted and precludes examining the effects of private intrafamily transfers, especially through extended family living arrangements which are known to be more important in the less developed countries. Furthermore, there is a question of ascertaining cause and effect, since different institutional arrangements may reflect different cultural values. For example, it may be true that social security benefits are different in societies that have different attitudes toward thrift; in particular, benefits may tend to be larger when the propensity to save is lower. While differences of interpretation are possible, the evidence still does not reject the hypothesis that social security reduces private real capital accumulation.

The most convincing studies of the effects of social security on private attitudes toward thrift would rest on detailed examination of individual consumption and savings behavior rather than on aggregates; but unfortunately such studies have been limited by the unavailability of data. Some well known earlier studies seemed to indicate that enrollment in pension plans actually increased savings in other forms,[12] a finding which might be explained by the obvious fact that those with greater propensities to save would naturally tend to select themselves into private pension plans. If so, the fact of enrollment would not be a causal factor at all. Recent reworking of the earlier data is consistent with that hypothesis; and a more recent study (by Munnell) has found a negative relationship between pension plan and other types of saving. This finding is also consistent with the asset substitution hypothesis.[13] Finally, surveys of beneficiaries by the Social Security Administration indicate little change in the private wealth-to-income ratio of retirees despite large increases in real social security benefits, which implies little effect of social security on private capital accumulation.[14]

In sum, the empirical findings provide weak evidence that social security has had a harmful effect on private savings. However, the findings are not strong enough to make definitive judgments about the magnitude of the effect.

SOCIAL SECURITY AND RETIREMENT BENEFITS

The effect and fairness of social security's work retirement test has had a long history of discussion and debate. The adversaries in the debate tend to line up with their commitment to social adequacy of the benefit structure and to individual equity. Those stressing equity tend to view social security as an annuity system, while those stressing adequacy tend to view it as a government transfer program and therefore play down its intergenerational and life cycle aspects. If the work income test actually does discourage labor force participation, it must also reduce the total resources devoted to market production and reduce measured, marketed output per capita. This possibility is similar to any adverse effects on private capital accumulation, since it reduces the total amount of market goods available to be distributed to members of society. In another sense, it is unlike the effects of reduced capital accumulation, both because effects on labor supply do not necessarily cumulate over time and because reduced employment and market activity permit greater consumption of leisure as well as the possibility of producing goods outside the market and in the home. Neither of the latter are counted in official national income accounts but represent real income nonetheless. To keep the issue in perspective, it is also important to remember that the total number of workers possibly affected is small in relation to the total labor force, perhaps 2 or 3 percent of all workers. These percentages are apt to grow, however, when the postwar baby boom approaches retirement after the turn of the century.

It is true that in the 1930s the work income test was hardly controversial, given the prevailing unemployment at the time. However, ambivalent attitudes toward the test are indicated by many, often erratic, changes in legislated work restrictions over the years, sometimes tending toward liberalization, other times toward restriction. For those retiring before age 72 the present test makes earnings of $2,520 exempt, with benefits withheld at the rate of $1 for each $2 above the exemption.

Over the years the work retirement test has been justified by appeal to the purposes and principles of social security, with social security viewed as insurance to replace earnings lost due to retirement and disability. One may wonder how insurance principles apply to events such as retirement which are not purely acts of nature but are partially, and in fact often completely controlled by the insured. While it is true that private pension plans place restrictions on employment with the previous employer or industry, they do not typically preclude working in other industries. Also, mandatory retirement provisions reenforced by social security retirement statutes have been justified as a gentle and humane way of surmounting subtle or explicit tenure provisions in employment contracts, and of clearing away deadwood in organizations. Yet why should such restrictions exist for the more casual type employments desired by the elderly? We have also seen above that the work retirement test does encourage private thrift, but only if the test actually does encourage earlier retirement than would otherwise occur. Finally, from the welfare standpoint, the test discriminates against those who have heavily invested in their own earning capacity rather than in nonhuman capital assets, since the test disregards sources of income other than earnings. The $1 for $2 reduction in benefits is equivalent to at least a 50 percent marginal income tax rate on earnings. It is a paradox of major proportions why here, as in other "welfare" programs, such high tax rates should strike the poor, whose major asset is their ability to earn in the labor market.

Again, the empirical evidence on the actual effects of the retirement test is mixed. Time series data do suggest the possibility of a strong detrimental effect, but it is difficult to isolate the effects of the work test alone.[15] Labor force participation rates of men 65 years of age and older have fallen from 48 percent to 22 percent from 1947 to 1974, and in recent years there has been an increased trend toward taking the early retirement option. Yet this is also a period of rising per capita income and increased enrollment in private pension plans, both of which would tend to work in the same direction.

Other evidence is available from survey data on individuals. Chief among these are statistical surveys of beneficiaries periodically taken by the Social Security Administration, which directly question beneficiaries on the reasons for their retirement.[16] While it is true that at current benefit levels many low-wage earners can actually increase their income by retiring, the overwhelming response to survey questions givens limitations of health and mandatory retirement provisions as the main cause of retirement. Still, in recent surveys the number of respondents has increased who state that they voluntarily retired to enjoy leisure. However, economists have always been suspicious of subjective data of this sort, because the interview technique may itself bias the answer.

The issue would be more settled if the subjective responses were confirmed by more objective observations of actual behavior; but studies based on objective data tend to reach rather different conclusions than those based on surveys. In a widely quoted study, Bowen and Finegan attempted to ascertain the objective factors determining labor force participation of men between the ages of 55 to 64, and extrapolated the results to men 65 years of age and older.[17] Their findings emphasized the importance of nonwage income in influencing the labor force participation decision, which naturally projects a very large response of retirement decisions to greater social security benefits. These results are questionable on several grounds. First, no direct evidence is presented for social security beneficiaries. Second, those in the 55-64 age group who had accumulated capital assets and had significant nonwage income may well have done so because they planned to retire early. If those who retired later had different tastes for leisure and work, or different opportunities, an extrapolation outside the actual sample would not be valid. Third, it is not apparent that a common structure would apply to both age groups because of differences in health, mandatory retirement provisions, and so forth, none of which were controlled in the study. Because it is based on the actual behavior of retirees, the best available study from the methodological point of view is by Boskin.[18] In addition to other interesting results, this study concluded that a $1,000 increase in social security benefits raises the probability of retirement by about 8 percent. This is the largest effect reported in the literature, but it should be viewed with caution because of a rather small sample; it is not clear, therefore, to what extent this result holds for the population at large.

Though the long-run effect of the earnings test remains uncertain, it seems probable that abolishing it would have small short-run effects on elderly labor force participation. Based on that assumption, the Social Security Administration estimates that abolishing the test would initially cost about $4 billion per year.[19] Most of this would go to those already in the labor force whose wage opportunities encourage them to go above the test limitations in any case.

One interesting conceptual difficulty with all studies of this problem is the treatment of work opportunities for the elderly. At the moment, and perhaps because of the work test, the market for elderly workers is quite thinly traded. Desirable and interesting jobs suitable for them must have relatively flexible and short work hours and are not widely available. Further liberalization of the earnings test is likely to have only minor effects on employment in the short run, until the labor market adjusts the supply of desired job opportunities to the demand for them.

INTRAGENERATIONAL ISSUES

So far we have discussed some issues related to intergenerational transfers and their possible effects on the total supply of market resources in the economy. We shall now conclude with a brief consideration of narrower issues arising naturally in the life cycle perspective adopted here, and relating to individual equity among members of the same generation.

The social security system may well redistribute lifetime income among members of the same birth cohort over and above any intergenerational effects. A glance at the payroll tax and benefit schedules obviously indicates that possibility. Viewed only as a mechanism for raising government revenue, payroll taxes are known to carry with them efficiency distortions that reduce the output potential in the economy. Moreover, the wage base limitations of the payroll tax make it regressive; it is a greater burden on the poorer than on the wealthier members of each generation. This fact has supported recent popular discussion about partially funding social security from general revenues. On the other side of the coin, the benefit schedule is progressive and highly "tilted" in favor of those with a history of lower average covered earnings. The fact that regressive taxes are paid during working years and progressive benefits received in retirement means that overall progressivity or regressivity of social security pensions can be determined only by examining their effect on lifetime income distribution. Useful summary statistics are available for this purpose; namely, the annuity value of social security pensions, or alternatively, the realized rate of return on social security taxes. It is also of some interest to compare these values with those available from the private market.

Several studies have undertaken such computations in recent years. Before turning the results, two major qualifications are necessary. First, as pointed out above, those retiring before the system is fully mature pay taxes for a briefer period than those covered close to the time of their first job. Since early beneficiaries receive full benefits, social security is an especially "good deal" for them. Hence, meaningful comparisons with private pension plans require examining situations where workers have been covered for the whole of their working life. Second, there are questions about the incidence of the payroll tax, which is nominally shared half-and-half by employer and employee. Despite widespread public confusion on this issue, economists agree almost universally that almost the entire burden of the tax falls on workers and that the tax is fully shifted to labor. The reason is that social security payroll taxes paid by employers add directly to labor costs in exactly the same manner as wage payments. Also, payroll taxes involve a *quid pro quo* in the form of accumulated retirement benefits similar to private pension credits and other forms of deferred compensation. Thus in computing the rate of return or annuity value per dollar of cost, it is inappropriate to use only the worker's share of the payroll tax as a base. It is much more nearly correct to attribute the entire tax to the worker, whoever nominally pays it.

Social security may also redistribute lifetime incomes among members of the same generation because its actuarial basis is not the same as the basis in private annuities.[20] For example, persons in high income classes typically pay the payroll taxes over a shorter period because schooling defers their entry into the labor force. They also have a longer life expectancy and collect benefits for a longer period. Moreover, exclusion of the employer tax share from the personal income tax base relatively benefits those with high income and high marginal tax rates. Lastly, upper-income persons gain relative advantage from the fact that benefits are free of personal income taxation.

Empirical evidence shows that on the average, covered workers can expect an annuity value comparable to what they can purchase in the private market.[21] But there are substantial deviations around the mean. Some are well known, such as the advantageous treatment of married couples with one working spouse, and need not be discussed. But the discussion above suggests there are other, more subtle, and systematic transfers. A recent study shows that essentially for the reasons given above, social security yields a higher rate of return for higher-income groups.[22] Another study of differential white and nonwhite experiences under social security illustrates the idea that the regressivity of the tax structure and progressivity of the benefits structure largely offset each other.[23] The average rate of return for nonwhites is larger than that for whites because average earnings of the former group are lower and the benefit schedule is sufficiently progressive to outweigh the regressivity of the tax. On the other hand, the average rate of return is larger for whites than for nonwhites with the same covered earnings record, because nonwhite life expectancy is shorter and the average benefit period correspondingly smaller.

In summary, there is strong evidence that social security does transfer incomes among members of the same cohort, as well as between generations. Some of these transfers tend to reduce income inequality; others tend to increase it. The best policy may be to adjust the structure to neutralize the intrageneration transfers in social security and to rely on other more welfare-oriented programs for redistribution within generations. But these changes will probably alter behavior in some ways. For example, the rate of return on social security taxes for higher-income persons could be reduced by making the benefit structure more progressive. Yet if the replacement ratio for those with low average covered earnings rises above present levels, the labor force participation of lower wage elderly workers may be even smaller.

CONCLUSION

It is apparent that much of the discussion and debate on social security has clarified issues and drawn out battlegrounds. But despite the virtues of rigorous theoretical argument for clarifying thought, most of the points at issue can only be resolved empirically, and here there is some distance to go. Certainly much progress has been made, especially in regard to some of the narrower technical questions such as those relating to rates of return on social security taxes. On the other hand, answers to broader questions of economic behavior, such as the effects of social security on private savings and labor force participation decisions, are much more difficult to answer. But a running start has been made. The available evidence does suggest that social security has some effect on those decisions, but hard analytical research in these areas is of very recent origin.

Given the extremely rapid growth of social security benefits and taxes, and the potentially enormous role they play in affecting our economy, we must demand more definitive answers in the near future.

VI

GEORGE F. BREAK

SOCIAL SECURITY
AS A TAX

The payroll tax burden. Social security and the Great Depression. Assurance vs. insurance. Effects of inflation, recession, and the birthrate on trust fund concept. Exemption of property income. Employee and employer "contributions." Payroll tax and unemployment. Benefits-received and ability-to-pay financing. General fund financing. Public acceptance.

Taxation of payrolls is so common in the United States that few respondents in a man-on-the-street interview would be likely to name it as a pressing public issue. Yet one must remember that the familiar phenomenon of smog escaped general notice until people began to choke on it—at which point the press publicized it as a "problem."

The smog analogy should not be pressed too far; but the growing bite that the payroll tax is taking, especially at the lowest end of the earnings scale, has become a growing concern.

One reason the issue has seemed abstruse—until recently debated almost exclusively in the arcane regions inhabited by professional economists—is that most minds identify the payroll tax almost entirely with social security and equate it with the premiums paid on medical or other insurance. This chapter will show why the public should reexamine that equation, which was never very accurate. It is already attracting a widening circle of attention among policymakers.

For those interested in the philosophical bases of government tax and expenditure policy, the custom of financing social security by a payroll tax offers an intriguing, multifaceted subject for intellectual analysis. It is also grist for the mill of the most pragmatic politician. In the federal tax structure, the social security payroll tax currently accounts for more than one-fourth of total tax collections, ranking second in importance only to the personal income tax. More urgent, however, is the fact that even at this collection rate it is barely keeping pace with the outflow from the trust funds that it feeds—i.e., with social security payments to the elderly, the disabled, and other beneficiaries of the system. While this country also levies other payroll taxes (notably for unemployment insurance), the following discussion will center primarily on the cluster of taxes earmarked for old age and survivors' benefits, disability benefits, and Medicare. The analysis will focus on the rationale for this method of financing social security, its effects on the general economy, and the impact it has on the workers whose earnings are taxed.

The main problem in the social security system is its attempt to achieve two goals with only one financing instrument. The goal of social insurance requires financing based on earned entitlements; the goal of social adequacy requires taxation based on ability-to-pay. Fundamental improvement in the system depends on designing social security finances with these distinct purposes in mind.

BACKGROUND

The U.S. social security system is relatively young. It was born in 1935 during the Great Depression and was conceived then as a kind of "social insurance." Although never intended to be subject to the strict actuarial standards used by private insurance programs—in which accumulated premiums are invested, individually accounted for, and contractually related on the basis of "equity earned" to the benefits later payable—the original old age and survivors' social security plan nevertheless was seen as a modified form of that concept. Workers were to pay a small percentage of their earnings up to a specified ceiling into a trust fund; their employers were to contribute an equal amount. The trust fund was later to provide benefits to those who had paid into the plan during their working lives, reached a designated age, and retired from the labor force. To qualify, one first had to earn coverage by employment and payment into the system for a minimum number of quarter-year periods. Even then benefits were to be paid to covered persons of retirement age only if they in fact did retire from the work force—payments being reduced or suspended entirely, according to a fixed scale, as long as employment earnings continued. Benefits were to vary within a range related to the worker's lifetime contributions into the system, although the formula was weighted to provide somewhat more generously for the lowest-wage earners.

As originally devised, therefore, the social security program was essentially predicated on insurance principles modified to provide a guaranteed minimum retirement income for all covered workers. By stressing the concept of "earned" benefit, it made a limited form of nationwide income protection acceptable even to conservatives wary of government encroachments into the private domain. It also had the great advantage of dissociating benefit payments from need, and hence from the "welfare" stigma. So important did these values seem in 1935 that despite the ravages of the Great Depression the initiating legislation called for accumulating payments in the social security trust fund until 1942 before any benefits were to be paid.

It was not long, however, before subsequent U.S. Congresses began to modify the conservative concept on which the 1935 act was based. In 1939 the social security program was fundamentally revised by amendments that stressed minimum income needs more than strictly earned entitlements. While the method of financing remained the same—1 percent deducted from the first $3,000 of a worker's earnings and matched by the employer—major extensions were made in benefits. Coverage for workers was broadened to include dependents and even survivors. Payments of benefits were to start not in 1942, but almost immediately, in 1940. Benefits were to be related to average earnings over a minimum covered period rather than to lifetime contributions into the system. *Assurance,* in short, was to replace *insurance* as the dominant principle of social security. This was a major shift. During the subsequent thirty years many more modifications in the system confirmed and extended this basic alteration of course.

A greatly broadened benefits schedule has, of course, required periodic increases in payroll tax rates (now 5.85 percent each for employees and employers) and in the level of earnings subject to tax ($16,500 in 1977 and indexed to keep pace automatically with wage and price rises). Many types of employment not originally covered have been added to the system, which in recent years has been extended even to the self-employed. Some vestigial remnants of the old concept remain, including the separation of the levy into the employer and employee "shares"; but a growing number of policymakers are beginning to join economists in perceiving the combination as nothing more than a tax on payrolls. And increasing scrutiny is being made of both the incidence and the economic effects of a high and growing tax on about 80 percent of the nation's total wage bill.

The subject is emerging from the pages of economic journals into general view largely because of the recent squeeze on the trust funds (now multiple) by the combined effects of inflation, recession, and a declining national birthrate. With the abandonment of any actuarial basis for the system, its solvency came to depend on maintaining a comfortable balance between incoming payroll tax payments and outgoing benefits. As in the case of a chain letter, the long-term balance could be assured by a growing influx of new participants into the system. This equilibrium, considered safe in 1935 and for many years following, looks far less secure for a population with a declining birthrate. Morever, the once unthinkable conjuncture of rapid inflation and widespread unemployment has added a more immediate complication. To satisfy the program's income maintenance goals, Congress has responded to inflation by raising benefit levels; but it has been reluctant to depress the economy further by increasing the payroll tax enough to keep pace with higher benefits. Thus outflow has been exceeding intake, and unless some adjustment is made, the trust funds could run dry within five years.

Congress will have to decide whether to raise the tax, or break with the established tradition of a self-financing system. In the past, Congress has departed from that tradition only in special circumstances—as when it extended coverage to new beneficiaries and agreed to fund benefits from general revenue. Given the tendency to regard income adequacy as the highest priority, it will become increasingly difficult for Congress to meet all social security needs of a gradually aging population by steadily pushing up the effective rate of a tax that many regard as highly regressive—i.e., one whose burdens steadily decline (as a percentage of family income) as income rises.

JUDGING THE REGRESSIVENESS OF THE PAYROLL TAX

Whether the regressive feature of social security financing is objectionable depends on one's view of the system's essential nature. If the payroll tax is seen as a payment for future benefit rights or entitlements, it is not the burden of the tax that is important, but the relation between current contributions and the value of future benefits. Under this interpretation the system is seen as a form of socialized saving, and the key questions concern expected rates of return for different family incomes. While determining these rates is complicated, there is no doubt their distribution is progressive, not regressive, in relation to family income.

Another redistributive feature of the system is the transfer of income from one generation to another. So far retirees have received benefits more generous than their contributions into the system have warranted. In part this reflects the steady growth in per capita real incomes and represents another progressive feature of the tax-transfer process. Each generation of workers, in other words, is richer than the last, and out of its greater ability to pay finances the retirement benefits of its less affluent predecessors.

A further aspect of the picture, however, is that the higher benefits are paid for by increasing payroll tax rates applied to a wage base with a steadily rising ceiling. Such intergenerational transfers are more controversial than those derived purely from increased affluence and would become more so if future economic growth rates should drop sharply, as some forecasts predict. In that event, new generations would not on the average be wealthier than the old and might well resist paying higher tax rates for other people's social security benefits.

Ironically, it is the very progressiveness of social security rates of return that gives rise to the alternative view of the system. This view holds that there is so little connection between contributions paid in and benefits to be received later that the program should be evaluated by the traditional tests of ability-to-pay taxation and needs-related benefit payments. By this view, unlike the first, the payroll tax should be considered separately from benefits and as part of the federal government's total tax system. This is in fact how the federal budget currently treats the tax, and this view leads naturally to the recently popular criticism of the program's regressivity.

The employee share of the payroll tax clearly has a regressive structure as it places a proportional tax upon the first $16,500 of all covered worker earnings. Since it does not tax income derived from property sources and is not imposed on earnings above the ceiling amount, its impact is generally regressive when measured against the entire income spectrum, although proportional within its own area of coverage. For wage income alone, the tax ceiling makes the tax rate regressive on the total wage income of all those earning more than the ceiling amount. The introduction of property income, however, complicates the pattern. Because property income tends to be a larger share of total family income in lower than in middle income ranges, payroll tax burdens can be mildly progressive, on average, over some part of the low and low-middle family income range. (See, for example, the second column of Table 1.) Above these levels, however, the employee portion of the tax is steadily and unequivocally regressive.

Whether the same can be said of the employer portion depends on whether its burdens are shifted to workers or to consumers or remain where they are placed by law—on business profits. The answer may be another example of Walter Heller's pronouncement that "there is an ironic but substantial inverse correlation between the degree of consensus among economists and the degree of public acceptance of their findings."[1] For most economists agree that the burdens of a payroll tax levied on employers are largely if not entirely shifted to workers. This may happen either because the tax makes money wages and fringe benefits lower than they otherwise would be, or because the tax pushes up both prices and profits while leaving wages unchanged in money terms. In the latter case, workers suffer a drop in real wages, the same money buying less than before, whereas profit receivers enjoy the same real income as though there were no employee payroll tax.

The theoretical conclusion that workers bear the burdens of a payroll tax legally levied on employers is supported by a growing body of empirical evidence.[2] Essentially it rests on the proposition that the amount of work provided by the employer is a function of the real wage rate; and when a component of that rate increases (as it does when a payroll tax is imposed), pretax employment levels can be maintained or reattained only if some other wage component declines or if prices rise enough to restore real wages to their previous level. One immediate reaction to a payroll tax increase may be a reduction in available work. But this situation is not likely to persist; rather, one of the mechanisms just mentioned will lower real wages and restore the pretax employment level. Even if long-term unemployment does result, workers as a whole will not avoid the tax burdens; the costs are simply shifted from those who remain employed to those who can no longer find jobs. The impact on workers as a group could be reduced only if some of them were to withdraw voluntarily from the labor market because they perceived the tax as a burden rather than a part of total wages allocated to saving for future contingencies. But even voluntary withdrawals would help support real wage rates in the face of payroll tax increases only for a time. In the longer run, business investment in plant and equipment would be affected, and these changes would eventually move real wages down by the amount of any employer-paid payroll tax.[3]

A special effect of an employer payroll tax levied only on wages up to a ceiling amount may be to discourage the employment of lower-wage workers. With a $15,000 wage ceiling, for example, one $30,000-a-year worker costs the employer half as much tax as two $15,000 workers. This feature of social security and unemployment payroll taxes, then, could widen the gap between unskilled and skilled wages and raise unemployment rates for lower-wage workers. How important these effects may be, however, has yet to be established empirically.

WORKER REACTIONS TO NEW VIEW
OF PAYROLL TAX INCIDENCE

The complexity of these economic effects generally obscures them from public view. Public reaction to increased social security benefits might change if those presently employed saw the employer share of the tax not as a contribution from someone else to their own future benefits, but as part of their own wage income going to current benefits for other people. Recognition of this might provoke more careful assessment of social security costs and benefits. Without such recognition, workers tend to overestimate the rate of return they can expect on their contributions, which they are accustomed to calculating as half their actual amount. The self-employed are less likely to make this error, since they pay 7.9 percent, or about two-thirds the combined employer-employee rate.[4]

A clearer perception of the employer portion of the payroll tax might encourage reevaluation by workers of their stake in social security, but it would probably have little or no effect on most of their personal economic decisions. It would be unlikely, for example, to induce them to spend more or less time working, since work/leisure choices generally are based on take-home, not pretax, income levels. Similarly, it is likely that the important choice between saving and spending is also primarily influenced by after-tax wages combined with expectations of future social security benefits.

TAX TREATMENT

The income tax treatment of the two "portions" also forms an important aspect of the question of who bears the burden of the payroll tax. Present treatment accepts the notion that they are different, since the employee "half" is included in the worker's statement of earnings and subject to personal income taxation, whereas the "employer share" is not. The fact that social security benefits are not subject to the personal income tax presumably rationalizes the inclusion of the worker share in the tax base at the time the "contributions" are earned. Recognizing that the employer share similarly belongs to this base would logically require a change in its present tax treatment. Theoretically, total consistency should also mean imputing to the worker's tax base not only the employer share of the tax but also any interest earned by the trust funds on contributions. This might be handled by keeping track of all contributions made by a worker, plus interest, and subjecting to later income tax only "excess" benefits—i.e., those exceeding the recipient's total contributions plus interest. Alternatively (and with equal consistency), the income tax might exclude all contributions paid into the social security trust funds from whatever source and then make all benefits taxable to recipients.

PROPOSED "REFORMS"

Growing criticism of the payroll tax as regressive and rising concern over the financial soundness of the social security system have stimulated interest in the reform of social insurance financing. As usual, however, "reform" means different things to different people—so that any change in national policy must involve basic decision-making about the optimal nature of the social security system as a whole. Should it preserve the broad outlines of a benefits-received program to which participants contribute to accumulate credits toward later benefit entitlements? Or should it be shifted to an ability-to-pay basis, with contributions closely related to taxpaying ability and benefits paid only to the needy? Or should it be essentially a dual system, combining a benefits-received income maintenance approach with ability-to-pay provisions for income support?

Choosing among these alternatives means more than clarifying the fundamental conception of social security; it is an essential first step in choosing any meaningful "reform" of social security taxation. For what makes sense under one conception of the system frequently makes none at all under the other. One cannot, in short, treat the revenue and the expenditures sides of a program of this sort as though they were unrelated. Hard choices must be made, and any changes in the method of financing social security must be consistent with decisions about what role the system is to play.

A BENEFITS-RECEIVED PROGRAM

A benefits-received social insurance system seeks compulsory allocation of some portion of family earnings to maintain income levels during periods of adversity (unemployment, disability, illness) and after retirement. Logically, it should be financed by a contributory tax bearing a close relation to the prospective income-maintenance needs of the worker's family. Under such a scheme, benefits during retirement, unemployment, and disability could quite justifiably be paid for by a proportional wage—or payroll—tax. The proportionality of the levy is fully in keeping with the higher benefits to be expected (i.e., needed) by higher wage earners. Taxing earning only up to a specified ceiling level is defensible if the program's aim is to provide basic rather than full income support. So far, the current social security tax is consistent with this concept.

Medical benefits open a new problem. Since medical expenditures bear little relation to family incomes, a policy of financing them by a wage tax has little to recommend it. A benefits-received approach to Medicare and Medicaid, therefore, is more logically implemented by a levy more closely resembling the premiums payable to private insurance plans—i.e., payments of specified amounts, related more to the number of persons covered than to income. Such a social insurance tax could be applied, of course, only to families able to afford it; others would presumably have their medical needs subsidized from general revenue.

The benefits-received principle provides a highly traditional, widely accepted basis for financing social security, though one almost impossible to preserve intact. In 1935 Congress followed numerous foreign parliaments in adopting a system based on earned benefits, received not as a matter of need, but of right. From the outset, however, as earlier pointed out, the U.S. system was adapted to serve more than that one goal, and the ambivalent nature which caused it to ply a zigzag course between contradictory principles was quickly revealed. In the Great Depression, scarcity of jobs was a major issue, and Washington was concerned not only with requiring employed persons to make provision for their own lean years, but also with speeding them out of the labor force as soon as they reached retirement age. Congress therefore mandated that benefits be reduced or eliminated entirely for anyone continuing to earn employment income. This requirement, which is inconsistent with the principle of earned benefits, creates problems for people over sixty-five who are willing and able to work; and it has come under increasing criticism as economic conditions have changed.

Congress's early adaptation of the benefits schedule to income needs rather than to earned entitlements was paradoxically applied to the expenditures side of the social security accounts without corresponding modification of the revenue side. This has resulted in particularly inequitable treatment of families with more than one wage earner. The assumption that a family has a single breadwinner plus one or more dependents made far more sense in the 1930s than it does today. Certainly that assumption lay behind the formula that the social security tax should be a flat percentage of all covered wage and salary income and that this should entitle the worker to specified benefits plus a proportionate share for each qualified dependent. As increasing numbers of wives have entered the labor force, the formula has become an anachronism, placing a disproportionate burden on families with more than one fully taxable income. Working wives get no tax reduction on their earnings, even though they gain at best a small increase in benefits over what their husbands' taxes would have entitled them to as dependents.

ABILITY-TO-PAY FINANCING

The obvious objection to a system based only on earned entitlements is that many families, even under the best of circumstances, cannot afford to finance their own retirement, medical, disability, or unemployment expenses. For them, at least, some ability-to-pay financing is essential, and many experts prefer to extend that principle to the entire system.

Full ability-to-pay financing would represent a drastic, and perhaps disastrous, change of the present system. Its attractions are seen by looking only at the tax side of the picture. The first two columns of Table 1 contrast the generally progressive structure of the federal individual income tax with the regressive structure of the social security payroll tax in 1975. Adding the taxes (column three) produces sharp tax increases at the bottom of the income scale, but only slight increases at the top. Column four shows the burden pattern, total revenues constant, of shifting social security financing from the payroll to the income tax. Advocates of this reform cite its significant shift of tax burdens from the bottom five to higher income classes (column five).

Many people conclude from this that general fund financing of social security would improve the distribution of federal tax burdens. However, it would also sever all connection between payments made into the system and benefits paid out. It has been proposed that general funding could maintain the appearance of a connection by making the payroll tax fully creditable against the employee's federal income tax liability, with excess payments being refunded in cash.[5] It is an open question how long such an accounting fiction could stand up against economic reality. Doubts certainly would arise over the desirability of using general funds to

Table 1

Effective Personal Income and Payroll Tax Rates Under Present Law Compared with Rates Under Payroll Tax Reforms Financed Through General Revenue, 1975

(percent)

	(1)	(2)	(3)	(4)	(5)	(6)
		Present Law		Proposed Reform		Reformed Payroll Tax with Allowance Phaseout[c]
Income Class[a] (thousands of dollars)	Income Tax	Payroll Tax	Total	Integrated Income and Payroll Tax[b]	Difference	Total
0-3	1.10	5.75	6.85	1.44	-5.41	2.12
3-5	4.87	5.32	10.20	6.37	-3.83	7.82
5-10	8.65	5.33	13.98	11.31	-2.67	13.17
10-15	10.76	5.55	16.32	14.07	-2.25	16.22
15-20	12.85	5.12	17.97	16.80	-1.17	18.28
20-25	14.69	4.46	19.15	19.21	+0.06	19.56
25-50	17.89	3.34	21.24	23.39	+2.15	21.73
50-75	24.83	1.67	26.51	32.47	+5.96	27.18
75-100	29.16	1.15	30.30	38.12	+7.82	31.17
100-500	33.90	0.60	34.50	44.33	+9.83	35.61
500-1,000	33.08	0.11	33.19	43.25	+10.06	34.35
1,000 and over	31.74	0.04	31.78	41.50	+9.72	32.90
All classes[d]	14.39	4.42	18.81	18.81	—	18.81

Source: Benjamin A. Okner, "The Social Security Payroll Tax: Some Alternatives for Reform," *Journal of Finance* (May 1975):574, 578. Simulations are derived from the Brookings Institution's 1970 tax file projected to 1975 income levels. Details may not add to totals because of rounding.

[a] Income is equal to adjusted gross income plus the excluded half of net long-term capital gains, dividend exclusion, and sick pay exclusion.

[b] See text for a description of how the taxes are integrated.

[c] Reform proposal includes an allowance of $1,300 and a $750 per capita exemption financed through general revenue. The exemption is phased out by $1 for every $2 of earnings above the basic allowance level and financed through general revenue.

[d] Includes negative incomes not shown separately.

pay government benefits to people in no kind of economic need. The doubts would stir reactions, perhaps initially including a tightening of the earnings test and a move to include benefits in the definition of federal taxable income. Such modest adjustments might soon give way to more fundamental changes, especially when federal budget pressures became tight. Why not (it would be asked) cut back on benefit payments to the affluent, to save money and free funds for programs supporting low income families?

Longtime contributors to the system—quite rightly—would see such proposals as abrogating the implicit contract under which they thought they had been providing for their own retirement and other needs. The political power of these past contributors might be strong enough to hold off for some time the integration of social security with other federal welfare programs. But as the years passed, the ranks of past payroll tax contributors would thin, and the principle of compulsory social insurance would be likely to give way to that of discretionary low-income family support.

REFORMS

Fortunately, it is not necessary to make the stark choice between social insurance and welfare. The present system, as already described, is a rather disorganized mixture of the two disparate modes. Future changes could simply aim at retaining the primary goals of both systems and sharpening the instruments suitable to each. In general, this would mean strengthening the existing benefits-received elements for middle and upper-income families, and introducing more ability-to-pay elements for lower-income families.

Restructuring the relative tax burdens on one- and two-earner families and removing, or at least liberalizing, the earnings test for retired people between 65 and 72 would strengthen the commitment to the benefits-received rationale for social security. Still greater commitment would come from tightening the currently loose connection between an individual's taxes and benefit entitlements. Separate accounts for each contributor (or couple) with contributions recorded in dollars of constant purchasing power plus interest would provide the ultimate in benefits-received financing.

A modest beginning in the direction of introducing more ability-to-pay elements for lower-income families was made in the Tax Reduction Act of 1975, which added to the federal individual income tax a refundable earned income credit for wage earners who have dependent children and incomes of less than $8,000 a year. The credit is 10 percent of the first $4,000 of wage and salary income; thereafter, the credit declines by 10 percent of income from any source over $4,000 up to $8,000. Designed to moderate the burden of the social security payroll tax on the working poor, the credit is fully deductible against federal income tax liabilities, with any excess claimable as a cash refund.

More sweeping ability-to-pay reforms would attempt to determine the reasonable ability of all low-income workers to provide for future economic contingencies. Those with lowest incomes presumably would be relieved of payroll tax burdens entirely; families immediately above those levels would be subject to reduced payroll tax contributions; and reductions would gradually be phased out at income levels sufficient to provide self-support for families of different sizes.

Several payroll tax reduction plans would satisfy these guidelines. One possibility would be to apply to the payroll tax the low income allowance and per capita personal exemptions currently used by the federal individual income tax. Personal exemptions are currently $750 per person or dependent, and the low income allowance is $1,700 for single persons and $2,100 for couples filing joint returns. Extending these features, which are periodically adjusted upward, to social security financing would eliminate payroll tax burdens on most or possibly all families with incomes below official poverty levels. These or similar payroll tax exemptions could be phased out gradually at higher family income levels, with the revenue loss made up by a transfer from the federal government's general fund. Such a transfer is preferable to higher payroll taxes on workers with wages above exemption levels (as is sometimes proposed), because general fund financing adheres much more closely to ability-to-pay principles.

The last column of Table 1 indicates the impact of one payroll tax change of this kind. The plan simulated provides a $1,300 basic exemption plus $750 for each dependent, with the allowance reduced by $1 for every $2 of earnings above exemption levels. Lost revenues are made up by a proportionate increase in the federal individual income tax. It is interesting to note how closely the combined income-payroll tax payments under this plan (column six) match the tax payments resulting from complete integration of the two taxes (column four).

Conclusion

Perspectives are bound to differ widely on a subject like the U.S. social security system—huge in scale, yet minutely personal to individual wage earners. This discussion may persuade some that the system's integrity must be maintained intact, the tax raised, and the trust funds rescued from peril. Others will conclude that the old structure must be scrapped in favor of general fund financing. Still others, preferring evolution to revolution, will prefer to see the old edifice not replaced but renovated.

While changes must be made, the social security system as we have known it has achieved a remarkable degree of public acceptance, despite its cost. That so costly a program could be financed by a heavy tax that provokes so little adverse reaction from taxpayers should give policymakers pause. Indeed, it could just be a consummation devoutly to be wished. Whether such a broad system could achieve such acceptance without earmarked financing is a question that advocates of change should consider deeply. The understanding that the tax is a personal investment in one's own future, however shakily grounded in fact, makes that levy palatable in a way that one not explicitly earmarked might not begin to approximate.

Who but the affluent themselves would be willing to pay taxes to provide benefits for the affluent? Preposterous as the logic may seem to some economists, a successful tax structure must be grounded in faith, and in a sense of equity. If the concept of earned entitlements inspires confidence and imparts a sense of equity, it cannot simply be dropped as a basic premise of social security without putting the whole structure in serious jeopardy.

VII

RITA RICARDO CAMPBELL

THE PROBLEMS OF FAIRNESS

Historical background. Benefit criteria: equity and social adequacy. Claims of inequity. Young workers v. older workers. Covered workers v. noncovered workers. Women v. men. Married women who work v. married persons who do not work. Single persons without dependents v. married persons with dependents. Working persons 65-72 years who work v. nonworking persons 65-72 years. Conclusion.

With 32 million individuals receiving social security benefits and 100 million individuals paying social security taxes at some time during the year, concern about whether the system is "fair" has greatly increased. Those who question whether their payroll taxes earn a "fair benefit" are young workers, women and especially married women who work, single persons without dependents, working persons 65-72 years, and some in the system who pay social security taxes as compared to those, mostly government workers, who are not in the system and who do not pay these taxes. A concept of "fairness," the goal of simplification under rapidly changing demographic conditions, and the actuarial imbalance argue for coverage of all individuals who work, equal treatment of men and women, and a long-run phasing-out of spouse's dependency benefits. Other recommendations to improve "fairness" are also made.

HISTORICAL BACKGROUND

Old-Age Survivors Insurance (OASI) was passed by Congress in 1935, requiring coverage and payment of taxes by employees, and matching payroll taxes by their employers. The program covered all workers under age 65 in commerce and industry, but not the self-employed, or employees of nonprofit organizations, or of governments—federal, state, and local. Retirement benefits were payable only to retired workers, not to their dependents. Social adequacy, rather than only the criterion of individual equity characteristic of private insurance, was achieved by weighting heavily retirement benefits of earners of low incomes.

In 1939, substantial amendments increased the "social " aspects of the system by adding survivor dependent benefits and by reducing the minimum coverage requirements. The latter were reduced from five years and $2,000 wages covered to only six quarters with either $50 each quarter or $300 of wages on which OASI taxes were paid during the three years preceding the worker's retirement or death. On the revenue side, OASI payroll taxes were imposed on workers over 65, but the earnings base remained at $3,000, and the payroll tax[1] rate (employee/employer) remained at 2 percent.

Over the past forty years the act has been amended many times to increase kinds and level of benefits, to expand coverage, and to increase the tax base and rates. Expansion of coverage and concurrent increases in the size of the labor force—together with the increasing OASI tax rate and base—until recently have yielded sufficient revenues to pay increasing worker, dependency, and survivor benefits to ever more persons while still maintaining a small, working trust fund. This has been accomplished in general by taxing the current working generations to pay benefits to the current aged. As of June 1976 the OASI trust fund has about $38 billion or about seven months of benefit payouts.

BENEFIT CRITERIA: EQUITY AND SOCIAL ADEQUACY

In more recent times social adequacy has replaced equity as the dominant influence on social security benefits, while charges of inequity have increased, as it has become more and more evident that people paying the same taxes are receiving different benefits.

The concept of individual or even family equity has almost disappeared from the social security system of benefits. Horizontal equity—that is, between members of an age cohort—increases as the relationship between benefits received and taxes paid approaches equality. Under this standard taxes paid by individuals within a given age cohort should have a direct relationship to benefit entitlements. This concept has been greatly eroded by a welfare concept of determining benefits in accordance with "social adequacy" at an undefined level of need. The concepts of equity and social adequacy thus are fundamentally competitive.

Additionally, some young working individuals claim that today there is little vertical equity between age cohorts because young workers are taxed higher amounts to support the social security benefits of today's retired generations, than persons in those generations paid.

As discussed in Chapters IV and V, most current retirees are receiving in benefits a large multiple of what they paid in taxes plus accrued interest, and some (e.g. low-wage earners or those with short covered earnings histories) receive a larger multiple than others. However, all current retirees receive more in benefits than the taxes paid plus accrued interest, while most young, healthy workers pay more in taxes than they will receive back in benefits. As the social security system matures, this intergenerational transfer or "vertical inequity" will decline in importance. Thus issues of horizontal equity are likely to become even more crucial unless corrected in the years ahead.

The increasing emphasis on social adequacy is responsible for the creation of additional social security benefits and trust funds— permanent disability benefits in 1954, and hospital insurance, Part A of Medicare in 1965. In addition, retirement and survivor benefits have been liberalized substantially, thereby creating new inequities.

CLAIMS OF INEQUITY

At the end of 1976 the following major groups complained about social security inequities:

1. Young workers v. older workers;
2. Covered workers v. noncovered workers;
3. Women v. men;
4. Married women who work v. married women who do not work;
5. Single persons without dependents v. married persons with dependents; and
6. Working persons 65-72 years who work v. nonworking persons 65-72 years.

All six groups complain that benefits are not fairly related to taxes. In addition to these groups, the homemaker who does not work for pay has a more general complaint: his or her work at home contributes to the well-being of the family, but society places no direct or imputed value on it. As a result, because it does not enter the national income accounts, it is not taxed. Without the tax, however, this problem seems to fall in a different category than the other claimed inequities discussed here. (For further discussion see Appendix A.)

Equity and adequacy are competitive as criteria, not complementary. For most of the program's history, the goal that benefits provide "adequate," minimal support was not the stated aim of social security. Rather, it was assumed that the program would augment private pension and insurance plans supported by individuals and groups, while other programs, funded from general revenues, would provide pure welfare benefits.

Welfare benefits in the United States have been steadily increasing in kind and amount. The latest of these programs, enacted in 1974, is Supplemental Security Income (SSI), which paid out about $5.8 billion in 1976. Other federal programs paid out sums totaling $17 billion for noncontributory programs such as food stamps and aid for dependent children, while Medicaid accounted for $8.3 billion and veterans pensions $3 billion. The total of all noncontributory payments equaled $22.5 billion, or about one-sixth of all "income assistance outlays."[2]

The total of all contributory and noncontributory programs for income assistance in 1976 amounted to $139.5 billion, or about one-third of the total U.S. budget. Nearly $73 billion of this was paid out by the social security program. Social security payments thus equal about one-half this amount, creating important economic effects on the distribution of income and on labor supply.

The fact that many people covered by social security today protest that the system is inequitable suggests the program has an important effect on the supply of labor and on saving—both of which could affect the size of the gross national product.

Young Workers v. Older Workers

The first amendments to the Social Security Act (1939) greatly reduced the number of quarters of covered earnings necessary for entitlement to pension benefits. Since 1939 "currently insured" has been defined as coverage of only six of the last twelve quarters of earnings before an individual turned 65 or died. The minimum amount of covered earnings required in each of these quarters was (and still is) only $50.

Being "currently insured" made it possible during the program's early years (1935-1947) for some older persons to retire after paying only a minimal amount of $6.00—that is, 2 percent payroll[3] taxes on $300. It is unlikely there were many persons in this particular group since most people earned more than $300 during the required period. But despite gradually increasing (OASHDI) tax rates—from 2 percent in 1947 to nearly 6 percent in the early 1960s, 8 percent by 1970, and almost 12 percent today—and despite steady increases after 1951 in the earnings base to which the tax rate is applied, older people retiring in the early years of the system have paid in far less on average than they or their surviving spouses now receive in benefits. (For details see the discussion by Parsons and Munro in Chapter IV.) This is true of all social insurance systems, and also of many company insurance plans which during the plan's early years try to cover older persons who had no previous chance for coverage.

By now, however, the United States social security system has almost fully "matured." Persons who retired in 1976 at 65 were 21 in 1932 (21 being the age when covered earnings are included in the computation for benefits). Such a person could have entered the system at age 23 years and worked for forty-two years or 168 quarters, when only forty quarters or ten years of coverage are required for full insurance. Those who retired early at age 62 in 1976 could have worked under the system and paid taxes for their entire working life. But, the minimum requirement for "currently insured" is still six quarters of coverage during the full twelve-quarter period before that person died or became entitled to benefits.[4]

In general fully insured persons are entitled to more benefits than those who are only currently insured. But from time to time Congress has amended the Act to permit older persons—for example those who became 72 before 1969—to have a special, lower minimum for entitlement to benefits. These arrangements definitely favor older people over younger.

Today the program makes benefits available to almost all aged whether or not they have paid in substantial amounts during their lifetime, with current benefits paid for by taxes on current workers. It is a "pay-as-you-go" or intergenerational transfer from today's younger workers to the retired aged. Furthermore, the act has been amended over the years to include more and more aged persons who had previously not been covered, as for example because of illness or because they worked in noncovered jobs such as in the federal government. The reason for noncoverage is immaterial to the fact that over the years the system has acquired huge liabilities on behalf of people who have not contributed substantially to the system.

Data on the rate at which benefits replace earnings (generally made available only by the Social Security Administration and its administrators) usually avoid pointing out that younger workers today are and will be paying higher payroll taxes partly because of these accrued liabilities to the already aged and near aged. This reflects the system's "social adequacy" concept, and as more jobs are covered—about 90 percent are today—the cost is spread over larger numbers of people. Thus it is good policy to have universal compulsory coverage, so that all working persons contribute to the needs of today's aged.

Because benefits are currently paid for many aged who paid little in taxes, healthy young persons entering the system today and who are taxed under today's legislation may, depending on relative increases in wage rates and in the cost of living, find that they can buy an annuity of the same amount for less than they now pay in social security taxes. The Social Security Administration points out that social security provides other benefits than an annuity, especially survivor benefits and permanent disability insurance and that whereas private pensions do not increase with inflation, social security benefits do. In June 1976, 4.5 million people were receiving permanent disability benefits under OASDI, of which about 3 million were disabled workers and spouses. But even including survivor and disability insurance, the healthy young male worker finds that he can get a similar package of total benefits at a lesser price in the private market.

It is hard to know if this is true for young women or not, because until recently it was very difficult even for professional women such as physicians to get any form of private permanent disability insurance. OASDI disability coverage has a tax rate and trust fund separate from the one supporting retirement benefits. It would be useful, therefore, to compare the price of the annuity and survivors' benefits as under declining term life insurance, with the employee/employer OASI tax rate and base and then make a separate comparison for permanent disability coverage. It may be that young women will come out better under social security for disability coverage than under private insurance, but it appears in general that female workers paying social security taxes do worse under the program than they would using the same money in the private market. A young woman who does not marry is in the same position as a single male in that dependency benefits will not likely be paid based on her earnings record. This may be offset partly by a heavier weighted benefit, since her earnings on average will be less, and unlike private insurance companies, social security will not actuarially reduce her annual benefit to reflect the fact that women live longer than men.

If the woman marries—as most women do—she may receive little or no extra benefit based on her own earnings record, because she already is entitled to a secondary or dependency wife's and/or widow's benefit, which is likely to be higher than a primary benefit based on her earnings. A woman is entitled to either a primary or secondary benefit, whichever is higher.

The disaffection of young persons with inequities in the social security system surfaced recently in the withdrawals from social security by employees of state and local governments—the only groups which can opt out of the system. By March 1976, 332 groups had withdrawn—involving mostly small groups and only some 50,000 employees. However, in December 1975 the State of Alaska gave notice of withdrawal, and New York City has given formal notification of termination of 112,000 of their total employment of 250,000. In so doing, New York City[5] announced it would save $183 million a year by buying into a private plan. The city of San Jose, California, announced after their withdrawal that they negotiated a package of benefits 25 percent higher and 3 percent cheaper than social security could offer.

For young persons with dependents who earn relatively low incomes, social security is still probably a better investment than its alternatives on the private market. On the other hand, new amendments which may gradually phase out dependency benefits and/or enact sizeable tax increases as well as correct the 1972 error which permits double counting of benefits may erase this advantage. If the benefit structure is not changed, and benefits are still tied to the cost-of-living index, with inflation young married males benefit under social security. Married women workers in general are worse off because they already have a dependency benefit. When earnings approach the maximum taxable base, young unmarried men can purchase equal protection in the private market for less money than the taxes paid. But there is also an unknown—the level of taxes young, future workers will pay to support scheduled benefits which, under conditions such as high inflation, will be higher than the earnings they replace.

Covered Workers v. Noncovered Workers

The more jobs are covered by social security—and about 90 percent are today—the more "social costs" of the system are distributed widely over the population. This fact provides a major argument for universal coverage, as well as an important basis for the "social adequacy" concept in the evolution of social security coverage. Social security administrators, however, generally omit from their otherwise acceptable explanation of social adequacy that no federal government job—from the lowliest clerk through the upper cabinet level and congressional representative—is covered, and therefore that those holding these jobs escape the part of social security taxes which help the already aged and those with much lower than average monthly lifetime earnings. People with the lowest average covered monthly lifetime earnings have a 122 percent weight on their benefits; and this weight, used in computing benefits, gradually and unevenly declines close to 20 percent as earnings approach the maximum taxable base. About 8.8 million workers, or 10 percent of the regular labor force of about 85 million in 1975, remain outside the system. Of these, 6 million are government workers, about 2.5 million federal, and 3.5 million state and local.

Forty-three percent of retired federal workers are drawing both civil service and social security retirement benefits. Knowledgeable government employees can get the latter by taking a minimal job— say, one evening a week—in covered work for only forty quarters over their lifetime and thereby collect both the weighted minimum primary benefits and secondary or dependency benefits—the latter based on primary benefits, deliberately increased to favor the low-wage earners in their regular jobs. By industry classification, men whose main jobs in May 1975 were in public administration— federal, state, and local government services—had the highest rate of multiple jobholders, 25 percent.[6] Of these, 14 percent had regular jobs in federal employment, with almost 12 percent in state and local.

Some federal employees have worked at different periods of their lives in covered work and thus have gained the required forty quarters of coverage. It seems extremely unfair that government workers can escape taxes intended to help other poorer persons maintain a minimum standard of living in old age, while receiving "windfall" benefits based on few tax dollars paid in. Despite the legal difficulties, both the Advisory Council on Social Security (1975) and the Consultant Panel (1976) recommended univeral coverage. However, the U.S. House Subcommittee on "Retirement Income and Employment" in December 1975 stated, without reservation, that "The Federal civil service has its own retirement system, which, unlike most private pension plans in the country, entirely replaces Social Security benefits" (p. 13). This disregard of the social adequacy concept in favor of individual equity for *federal* government workers but not others makes it difficult for knowledgeable persons to accept increases in their payroll taxes, knowing that federal workers are exempt and that state and local employees can choose not to pay. If all government jobs were covered, the system's short-term cost would be reduced by 0.70 percent of taxable payroll and the long-term cost by 0.25 percent; OASDI's annual revenues would increase immediately by almost $8 billion.

This chapter deals only with the general concept of fairness, or the balancing of equity and social adequacy. Therefore, we must avoid arguments of whether a particular group, such as a local government employee group, should remain in or out of the system. It is clear, however, that the group's age and sex composition and the marital status of its women would greatly influence the analysis for any particular group. In general, the great advantage of the Social Security System for even young individuals is that it provides for "vesting." However, the new federal rules on private pensions (ERISA) require minimum vesting rights, and this advantage has therefore been reduced.

Women v. Men[7]

Because the Social Security Act has added survivor and dependency to retirement benefits and because the act assumes that all married women and widows are dependents of their husbands, wives and widows automatically receive secondary[8] benefits without proof of need, while husbands and widowers are required to prove need or economic dependency, defined as receiving one-half of their support from their wives. Depending on one's orientation, this is inequitable, against women as earners and against men as beneficiaries. If the Equal Rights Amendment passes, the provisions of social security that provide differently for men and women would have to be changed. Meanwhile on 19 March 1975 the U.S. Supreme Court ruled in *Weinberger vs. Wiesenfeld* [9] that a male parent whose wife was "currently insured" under social security and died in childbirth was entitled to the same survivor parent's benefit that a widow with child would receive if her husband had similar social security coverage and died. The act has no provision for a father's benefit, but the Social Security Administration has issued guidelines to pay a father's benefit in accordance with the court's ruling.

Most secondary benefits cover both men and women, but for all categories of secondary benefits the man must prove that one-half of his support comes from his wife, before he is entitled to collect on her wage record. Since the passage of the act some forty years ago, women have entered the labor force in large numbers. If the ERA amendment passes and/or the Supreme Court interprets all differences by sex in the entitlement rules for social security benefits as unconstitutional, then the Social Security Act would have to be amended.

One recent advisory group recommended that the one-half support dependency requirement be eliminated, and that the entitlements to secondary benefits be made the same for men and women.[10] Because of the potential high costs of this recommendation, it recommended that simultaneously a pension based on non-covered work should affect entitlement to secondary benefits in the same way that a primary benefit does.[11] If men, as women do now, were to receive a spouse's or surviving spouse's benefit without proof of dependency, costs would increase. It would be inadvisable to require that women, as men do now, prove dependency, because this would increase both the welfare aspect of the program and also administrative costs. Persons who have earned a private pension are generally not in need, and this provides a simple but incomplete means test. If such a test were effective immediately, it would reduce secondary benefits for those working wives who are approaching retirement and are eligible for pensions from non-covered work.[12]

I prefer universal coverage and a gradual thirty-year phase-out of the secondary retirement benefit of wife and husband, and retention of all other benefits. My preference for a gradual phase-out assumes that the courts will require equal treatment of men and women and, therefore, high anticipated costs of secondary spouses' benefits to men resulting from the great increase in working women. Additionally women by working in covered employment are obtaining their own primary benefit. Also, I believe that whenever benefits are drastically reduced, a warning period of several years should be given, to protect persons who relied on receiving certain retirement benefits and may be caught unprepared.

Phasing out the secondary retirement benefit over a thirty-year period and additionally the secondary surviving spouse's benefit over a fifty-year period in my view, would be even more desirable, if the latter were politically viable. This is because it would also reduce substantially the long run actuarial imbalance of the OASI trust fund that now exists and also prevent a greater one from occurring when all dependency benefits based on men's and women's earnings are treated the same.

The number of women working continues to grow, as the number of years men work on average continues to decline. Moreover, it is important to consider that there have been great increases in type and expenditures of government welfare programs, over the past forty years. A gradual phase-out of *all* spouse benefits coupled with universal coverage might be the best solution to solve the major inequities, including that of single persons, and also to reduce much of the financial imbalance.

Married Women Who Work v. Married Women Who Do Not

Married women who work as wives are entitled at age 65 to one-half their husband's primary benefit (or at age 62, to a reduced amount); and on his death after retirement she can claim a widow's benefit equal to his primary benefit. As a result, many married women work and pay social security taxes but collect no additional pension benefit. The law counts first their "assumed dependency benefit" and increases it only if (and by the amount) the primary benefit on their own earnings record is higher. In practice, therefore, married women receive primary or dependency benefit whichever is greater, but not both.

One important reform of social security would ensure that single-earner and two-earner couples with comparable covered earnings would receive equivalent benefits. The Advisory Council on Social Security turned this reform proposed by its subcommittee on the treatment of men and women down as follows.

> The Council does not endorse the principle of providing benefits based on a married couple's combined earnings. A basic rationale for such proposals is that couples who have paid similar contributions should get similar benefits. However, in an earnings-related social insurance system, such as social security, benefits are not directly proportional to contributions. Further, the Council notes that there is a point beyond which it is difficult to justify complex exceptions to the social security law in the interest of providing benefits in relation to contributions for special groups.[13]

One way to avoid complexity is to permit married couples where both individuals work in covered jobs to combine their earnings up to the taxable base at the time of employment in computing their social security benefit. In 1975 the base was $14,100; in 1977, it is $16,500. Especially with low-income earners the uneven weighting of benefits creates the anomaly that a two-worker family can receive lower benefits on retirement than a one-earner family with an otherwise identical earnings record. Such a proposal is limited in that it would not help working couples where either person's earnings exceeded the base, and it would help two-worker couples to a lesser degree, the more their total earnings exceeded the base.

In addressing these and other proposed reforms, it is important to avoid "tinkering" but instead try to restructure social security into a logical part of the U.S. total system of taxes and social benefits. There are hundreds of thousands of couples—the precise numbers are not known—where both the husband and wife work, earn relatively low wages, and pay a tax on those wages; but when they retire at age 65, they receive not more but *less* than other couples where only the husband has worked and earned the equal of the two-worker family's combined wages. For example, a husband with average, annual earnings of $4,000 and a wife with average, annual earnings of $4,000 each receive $228.50 a month on retirement at age 65 or a monthly total of $457.00. This is $17.50 less than the $474.50 or one and one-half the monthly primary retirement benefit payable to a married worker with average, annual earnings of $8,000 and a spouse who has not worked in covered employment.

Consider the following, more general example: In Family A, the wife works and earns 40 percent of the family income each year, and the husband 60 percent; in Family B, the wife does not work. Since the social security program began, the annual earnings of the two families are equal and year-by-year are equal to the maximum, annual earnings tax base which is also used to compute benefits. Assuming all four individuals are 65 during the first six months of 1975, the husband in Family A would receive $226.50 monthly benefit and the wife, whose earnings were considerably less, $179.60, for a total monthly retirement benefit of $406.10. In Family B, where the husband alone has worked, he and his wife would receive a much greater monthly retirement benefit—the husband's primary of $316.30 plus one-half of this amount ("rounded") or $158.20 (a seconday benefit) of his "presumed dependent" wife, or $474.50 in total. For each year that Family B receives retirement benefits, it would receive $820.80 more (before automatic adjustments for inflation) than the two-worker Family A.

Such anomalies inhere in the present benefit structure. I believe, therefore, that retirement benefits should be paid on an individual basis as are the social security taxes now being collected. To argue that working, married women should not only contribute in large measure the "social" benefits under social insurance, but also in a family unit actually receive less than if they had never worked at all nor paid taxes is ethically unacceptable.

Those who argue otherwise fail to recognize the impact of the system on the increasing numbers of married women who work generally for low wages and pay OASDI taxes sometimes in preference to going on welfare or to avoid going on welfare when they are older. Many of these women pay higher social security taxes than income taxes. Many of the 22 million married working women (and generally also their husbands) are highly critical of the program because they know that on retirement or widowhood they will not receive any more benefits than if they had never worked and paid taxes during their lifetime. They may know that they have protection for dependent children and for long-term disability but feel that these tax payments are high "premiums" for such insurance. Since the vast majority of these women bear and raise children, they contribute to society in ways beyond those of most single persons.[14]

Married women make an important contribution to family earnings, and most work out of necessity.[15] In March 1975, 72 percent of working wives were working full time and the majority had husbands earning annually less than the "intermediate budget" for an urban family of four of $14,000 before taxes. Some people regard working married women as a "special group"; but the fact is that the majority of married women work at least the ten years required for "full insurance" under social security. The "special group" is the minority of married women who have not worked ten years during their lifetime.

Imputing earnings for homemaker services would raise serious questions of equity and administrative feasibility, but another reform would help "all regular low-paid workers," which includes many homemakers. The Advisory Council's Subcommittee on the Treatment of Men and Women reasoned that women working full time have median earnings only 57 percent of men working full time, and therefore more women are in the group of workers referred to under the special minimum benefit requirement as the "regular, low-paid worker." Moreover, many women work 30 hours a week, 50 weeks a year, selling in retail stores because it is advantageous to their employers to hire women this way rather than pay overtime for evening and weekend hours. To deal with this problem it has been recommended that the entitlement requirement be reduced by one-quarter to one-sixth of the prevailing tax base, which would have reduced the 1977 requirement for a special minimum benefit from $4,125 to $2,750 annually. That special benefit is equal to $9.00 times the number of years of social security coverage exceeding ten years, up to a maximum of thirty years.

After the Advisory Council reported, a task force report on *Women and Social Security* . . . , a Working Paper for the Senate's Special Committee on Aging, was issued in October 1975. Most members of the task force were former, upper-level, federal government employees but also included the Director of the AFL-CIO's Social Security Department and Duke economist Juanita Kreps. Their working paper recommended far more extensive liberalization of benefits, without attaching cost estimates. They proposed removing the dependency test for the husband or surviving spouse's benefits which are dependent on the wife's covered earnings but without offsets. The working paper also recommended correcting retroactively the inequity to men created by a difference in the computation in the benefits of males retiring from 1954-1974—a proposal which Congress had already considered in the 1972 amendments, and which was eliminated prospectively. They also proposed reducing from twenty to fifteen years the duration of a marriage necessary for divorced persons to claim benefits based on their spouse's earnings record, and would allow additional dropout years above the five years of low earnings now in the law for computation of benefits. Lastly, in order to make benefits of single workers (two-worker and one-worker couples) more equal, the task force proposed to increase all primary benefits by one-third and reduce spouse's benefits one-half to one-third of the primary benefit.

These recommendations and others would be very costly, but cost estimates were not supplied. In testimony, Commissioner of Social Security James Cardwell estimated that the last proposal alone would cost $9 billion in the first year of enactment. It is interesting that during congressional committee testimony, Senator Percy suggested that future increases in spouse's benefits might be made only if the spouse could prove dependency.

In August of 1976, a Consultant Panel on Social Security to the Congressional Joint Committee took an entirely new approach in trying to give greater equity to families where both husband and wife worked and paid social security taxes, yet often received no more and sometimes even less than where the wife did not work and paid no taxes. That panel's report defined the criterion for equity as "family equity," not "individual equity." This resulted in a complicated proposal which I do not think is administratively feasible since married individuals are of different ages, retire at different times, and are tending to higher divorce rates, often involving several marriages. Lastly, the question of "family equity" is confused by new life styles that are emerging in our more permissive society. Because of these socioeconomic changes and others already mentioned, such as the increasing number of women working and increasing individual life expectancies, a long-run, viable aproach requires that both benefits be paid and social security taxes be collected on an individual basis.

This approach would eliminate administrative difficulties inherent in trying to define "family benefit."

Single Persons Without Dependents v. Married Persons With Dependents

Over the years, single persons have protested that they pay the same social security tax as do married persons whose spouse and other dependents may collect upon retirement and/or death. In partial response, a dependent's parents benefit was added as early as 1939; but this reform does not permit single persons, whose parents usually have died before they retire, to gain from their earnings record anything close to the benefits that may be collected by a married person with spouse and sometimes a dependent child, or by a surviving spouse. It is difficult to find a solution acceptable to a majority, to reduce or eliminate this inequity. One possibility is to permit a dependency benefit for close relatives other than parents who had lived for a significant number of years with a single covered person prior to preceding retirement or death of that person.

My proposal to phase out a spouse's retirement secondary benefit would also reduce this inequity, but this particular argument for that proposal does not have a wide following. A more widely held view is that singles should contribute especially to dependent children's benefits and that although excess contributions could not be clearly earmarked for that purpose, an economic society, like a biological society, has responsibility for continuing its existence—and therefore, care of its young.

Working Persons 65-72 Years Who Work v. Nonworking Persons 65-72 Years

The social security primary benefit is a retirement benefit, and therefore, in order to collect it, a person is expected to retire from his existing job. If an otherwise entitled beneficiary is under age 72 and earns more than the annual exempt amount, his benefits are withheld at the rate of $1.00 in benefit for each $2.00 in earnings above that amount. The exempt amount is related to the earnings base and automatically increases with the annual increase in average earnings. Before 1954, earnings in noncovered work were not counted in the retirement test, but since that date all income from work is included and the earnings test is applied on an annual basis. Thus an individual may earn far above the annual exemption during two months of a year and collect social security monthly retirement benefits during the other 10 months if he does not perform any "substantial" service in self-employment during those months. It is thus possible for individuals on a company board of directors to receive an annual, lump sum payment exceding the annual exempt amount and collect retirement benefits in each of the other 11 months. The Advisory Council and the 1976 Consultant Panel both recommended that the retirement test be corrected so that the monthly measure be eliminated and applied solely on annual earnings.

The claimed inequity of the retirement test is probably the most political of all social security issues in terms of the high number of legislative bills dealing with it, the heated congressional arguments, and the amount of congressional mail protesting it. Current data are limited on why people retire, the effect of the earnings test on retirement, and the effect the act itself has on the retirement age. Those who argue against the retirement test point out that persons who continue to work in covered employment add to the system's income since they still pay social security taxes on their earnings. Also these older workers contribute to the national income, and thus increase the base on which personal and corporate income taxes are levied.

Those who argue for the retirement test point out that the social security system was initially founded to provide benefits upon loss of earnings and that if one has not retired one has not lost earnings. Moreover, during periods of unemployment, some claim that early retirement of the aged creates more jobs for the young. In a sense, this ignores that structural unemployment connot be eliminated in this fashion and also that monetary and fiscal policy are better methods of dealing with cyclical unemployment. Proponents of retaining the retirement test argue that it is not a "means test" nor is social security a welfare program because it does not take into account income from other earnings as interest, rent, and dividends. Lastly, of course, they argue that not paying benefits "saves" the system a lot of money.

One resolution of the problem would be to eliminate the social security tax on earnings of individuals 65 to 72 years of age and also—to make up the financial loss to the system—to impose the income tax on social security benefits received by the aged. Currently the aged have an automatic double exemption under personal income tax and regardless of income level do not pay taxes on social security benefits. This proposal would affect primarily the middle and higher income groups of the aged.

CONCLUSION

The United States is in a period of falling birthrates. In 1975 and 1976 the ultimate fertility rate was at 1.8 children per woman, or below the replacement rate (2.1) of the population. The 1976 Bureau of Labor Statistics projections of the percentage of women in the labor force by 1990 exceed the OASI's Trustees 1974 projections, which were used by the Quadrennial Council. These recent BLS 1976 projections as a percent of all women in given age brackets are much higher: 75 percent of all women 20-24 years; 63-64 percent of women 25-44; and 60 percent of women 45 through 54 years.[16] As labor force participation by women increases, birthrates fall. Over 90 percent of women today work for pay during different periods of their life. To ignore socioeconomic trends when making projections is foolhardy.

Largely because of the increase in the numbers of married women who are working, the system has been able to increase benefits without incurring even greater actuarial imbalances. Part of the increases—both in type of benefits and amount—have been financed by increases in both the tax rate and in the level of the tax base, as well as the expansion of covered occupations and the increasing employment level of a growing population. But increased benefits have also been paid for by the largely unpredicted increase in the percentage of married women who work, who pay the same taxes on their earnings as do others in covered employment, but who collect on retirement or widowhood only their primary or secondary benefit, whichever is higher. Thus taxes paid on their earnings records have created a large pool of tax monies available to support expansion. Eventually, however, the percentage of married women who work will level out; and this annual, additional source of revenues will dry up.

More than ever before individuals are entering the labor force later in life, such as those who go to college and train for professional jobs. And many leave the labor force earlier, or at a younger age, because of the inducement of a social security benefit at age 62 and the availability of private pensions. Trade union contracts of the United Automobile Workers, Steel Workers, building trades, communications workers and many in the insurance sector provide for early retirement at age 60 years or even 55, after fifteen years of service. Also, life expectancy is increasing. Thus, one can anticipate that thirty years hence, when World War II's excess babies reach retirement age and the impact of the falling birthrate of recent years is felt, the year 2005 will be just the beginning of a decline in the ratio of workers to nonworkers. Under these circumstances thought should be given on how to restructure incentives to encourage persons to work beyond age 62 and even beyond age 65. To continue, through legislative amendments, "tinkering at the edges of what was originally in 1935, a rather simple program" will create more inequities without solving the old inequities. The social security program is now so complex because of its many amendments that even well-informed persons do not understand it. The problem of restructuring social security within the present tax structure and welfare programs developed over the last forty years deserves attention for reasons of both efficiency and equity.[17]

VIII

CARL V. PATTON

THE POLITICS
OF SOCIAL SECURITY*

The original intent. Explicit changes. What do we think we have? Political implications. The special stake of the Social Security Administration. The importance of public misperceptions. Short range proposals. Mid-range proposals. The long term. The question of general revenues and the anomalous positions of conservatives and liberals. Imminent changes. Immediacy of the "long term" problem. The political, social, and economic risks of inaction. Conclusion.

Since the social security system was founded in 1935, politics has always been the governing influence on policy. For most of its history, public misunderstanding of the system has led to perceptions only of program benefits, rarely of program costs. These perceptions have recently begun to change, and many past political benefits associated with the program now threaten to become

*I am grateful to Lawrence Chickering for his many suggestions which helped shape this chapter. I also wish to thank Barry N. Checkoway, Albert Z. Guttenberg, Andrew M. Isserman, and Gretchen West-Patton for their comments on earlier versions of this paper.

liabilities which may threaten the very basis of the program. If so, policymakers may be forced to solve the long-term financing problem before they are ready to do so. The funding crisis is pushing a reluctant Congress to reexamine questions long regarded as political suicide. Whatever comes of these deliberations, politics will continue to be the largest single influence on policy.

In the past the major political factor in policy was the ease with which Congress could increase benefits for a relatively small body of recipients by spreading the burden of taxes among a much larger working population. A combination of inflation and demographic changes in the population as a whole has changed the political climate; further tax increases have become politically difficult, and politics is forcing social security policy in new directions, still to be determined.

The political climate surrounding social security has rested on widespread public misconceptions about the program. Fundamental reforms must therefore depend on increased public awareness of what social security really is, and how it got that way.

THE ORIGINAL INTENT

Social security was originally established as a modest retirement system for employees of private industry. To build support, proponents described it as a private insurance program. "Contributions"—in fact, taxes—would be deposited in the Old Age Reserve Account, and all workers would eventually participate. In concept, benefits would relate to contributions. Benefits would be specified by law and paid to retirees who earned the right to them. By formula, earnings plus work experience would determine the retirement payment. Originally, benefits were not to be determined by need. Since the program would be contributory (on the belief that individuals are responsible for saving for their old age), it emphasized the relationship between work and benefits. Moreover, benefits to be received after retirement were seen as a shift of income from the present to the future, replacing a certain proportion of a worker's pre-retirement income.

Though the system was originally established as a retirement insurance program, it was clear from the beginning that its reality would be very different. Program objectives made any substantial adherence to the insurance purpose impossible; redistribution inhered in the original concept—which was primarily to transfer money from younger, richer generations to older, poorer ones, with the transfer perhaps declining over time.

The logic of this purpose becomes obvious from circumstances surrounding enactment of the program. First, it was enacted during the depression both to provide for persons in retirement, and even more important, to remove older persons from the work force. Second, the designers of social security, President Roosevelt's Committee on Economic Security, realized that if the system was to be a purely self-sustaining insurance program, it would be years before retirement payments of any size could be made.

A pure insurance program, actuarially sound, would not achieve program objectives. Its limited funds would neither encourage older persons to retire from the work force, nor provide for even prudent savers whose retirement savings had been destroyed. The program's insurance function was therefore compromised from the beginning and the committee proposed that retirement incomes exceed the actuarial value of contributions. The extent of the "compromise" is indicated by the fact that initial recipients received benefits fifty times greater than their contributions plus interest. (See Chapter IV for details.)

Compromising the insurance goal was politically easy. Transfers to the elderly were (and are) widely supported, and in the program's early years only a small proportion of the population would receive benefits. At the time there were nearly ten people in the labor force for every person above age 65. The immediate expense (per taxpayer) would be small; but the gain (per recipient) would be large.

Roosevelt's analysts knew the program's eventual cost. The retirement age of 65 was selected to remove as many persons as possible from the labor force while keeping the program within tolerable limits.[1] Roosevelt's analysts originally called for a 1 percent tax rate, split evenly between employee and employer, slowly increasing to 5 percent (1 percent every five years) during the program's first twenty years.[2] Older persons would receive benefits exceeding their contributions, paid by advances from younger workers who would not draw pensions for many years. The advances were to be repaid with interest from general revenues, beginning about 1965.

When Roosevelt learned of the $1.4 billion deficit expected in 1965, he first thought there was a mistake, because he assumed the system would be self-sustaining. When told the figures were correct, he insisted the program be changed.[3] Initial tax rates were then doubled to 1 percent for both employers and employees, and the maximum combined rate was to increase to 6 percent by 1949. The committee's actuary estimated the revised tax schedule would make the program self-sustaining until at least 1980 and would create a reserve of nearly $50 billion.[4]

The program passed both houses of Congress during the week of 5 August 1935, and was signed by the President on 14 August. It established the basic federal plan of social insurance for the aged, provided for a federal-state system of unemployment insurance, and authorized federal matching grants to the states for the poor aged, the blind, and dependent children.

Compared to other programs advanced at that time, the social security program was rather conservative.[5] The administration therefore could argue that unless conservative opponents accepted it they might later have to accept something more radical.[6]

The initial Social Security Act emphasized individual equity, and maximized political support by arguing that workers would get their money's worth from their contributions. In Roosevelt's mind social security would be a cornerstone for a larger program, to be supplemented by private savings and pension programs.

EXPLICIT CHANGES

The first explicit shift away from the insurance principle occurred in 1939, one year before the first benefits were paid. At that time benefit levels exceeding actuarial value of contributions were established, and the system was placed on a pay-as-you-go basis. Current workers were to pay for the benefits of retirees, under the implicit agreement that tomorrow's workers would do the same.

Only a small trust fund would be maintained under this arrangement to help level fluctuations between income and outgo. Solvency would be ensured by tax rates meeting benefit levels, not, as in private pension schemes, through accumulation of a fully-funded investment account.

The original insurance scheme was also modified in the benefit formula, which was weighted toward lower-income workers, and which provided secondary benefits for dependent wives even though they had never worked. By abandoning the concept of a fully funded, actuarially sound program and by unlinking taxes and benefits, the basis was provided for a program *thought* to be insurance but in fact a redistributive system of transfer payments.

The Advisory Council which drafted the 1939 changes argued for the use of general revenues on grounds that the nation as a whole would benefit from this broadened scope of social security.[7] Congress did not agree, however, and froze the 1 percent tax rate until 1943 to avoid burdening a depressed economy. While Roosevelt argued for tax increases to protect the long-term actuarial soundness of the program, seven times between 1942 and 1950 Congress postponed tax increases, citing trust fund surpluses. In 1944 Congress froze the tax rate over a presidential veto and authorized an appropriation from general revenues if needed to keep the program solvent. Congress repealed the authorization in 1950, in response to pressure to protect the system's actuarial soundness.

Nonetheless, the shift away from strict insurance continued. In 1950, amendments granted special wage credits to World War II veterans and continued benefits to the survivors of veterans who died within three years of discharge. Dependents' pensions for wives under 65 caring for an eligible child were added, along with pensions for husbands of female retirees and for divorced mothers. In 1957 pensions for workers disabled after reaching age 50 were added; in 1958, benefits for dependents of disabled workers; and in 1960 disability benefits were extended to persons below age 50.

In the early 1960s, Congress and the administration restated the official position of the 1950s: that social security ought to be self-supporting. Nevertheless, the 1965 amendments extended hospital insurance, to be paid out of general revenues, to all who reached age 65 regardless of whether they qualified for monthly social security benefits. Further, an amendment to the Tax Adjustment Act of 1966 provided benefits to be paid out of general revenues for persons who would reach age 72 before 1968 and would otherwise be ineligible for monthly benefits. More recently, in 1972, disabled workers under 65 were made eligible for Medicare, and an inflation adjuster was added to monthly benefits.

The shift of policy toward a social welfare program has been continuous and is evidenced in several ways. Not only do some persons receive benefits for which they have paid no taxes, but social security benefits have increased more rapidly than the consumer price index, and social security payments have reduced the percent of the elderly below the official poverty level.

Despite policy changes increasing the transfer purpose at the expense of insurance, it is too simple to say, without qualification, that the system has moved away from the original concept. In terms of dollars—the ratio of benefits to contributions—transfer payments were at their peak in the early years of the program, when the relatively few retirees received large benefits (at least in relation to what they paid in). Over the life of the program, the ratio of benefits to contributions has declined substantially, because recent beneficiaries tend to have a longer history of contributing than their predecessors. Recent policy emphasizing transfers has not so much changed the original concept; it has merely mitigated the natural tendency of the transfer element to disappear.[8] The important point here is that until recently the transfer element has been the primary political goal of social security, but now it is losing its dominance.

WHAT DO WE THINK WE HAVE?

Most Americans think social security is a contributory insurance system from which they will receive benefits after reaching age 65. Many people believe their social security number is a retirement deposit account number—like a bank account number—which identifies a specific accumulation of funds.

The Social Security Administration does little to discourage this impression. The booklet I received with my social security card states: "Your card shows the number of your social security account. It is necessary to identify the account as belonging to you."[9] Careful reading will indicate that the account is used to record earnings upon which benefit levels depend. Other documents imply that employee contributions are accumulated in an earmarked trust fund. A 1976 Social Security Administration booklet thus states:

> The basic idea of social security is a simple one: During working years employees, their employers, and self-employed people pay social security contributions into special trust funds. When earnings stop or are reduced because the worker retires, dies, or becomes disabled, monthly cash benefits are paid from these funds to replace part of the earnings the family has lost.[10]

Although technically correct, this statement gives the impression that a worker's "benefits" are financed by his own "contributions." The reality is that current taxes are being used to pay current benefits; and while some persons may recognize that nonvoluntary "contributions" are taxes, most others believe (as the social security booklet encourages them to do) that they are "building protection for themselves and their families" as if they were paying into a private annuity program.

Despite this impression, future protection has in fact little to do with current contributions. It depends, rather, on the willingness of future generations to continue paying taxes. Moreover, over time policy changes increasing the transfer goal also increase the distortion between contributions and benefits.

The widespread belief that people put away money through the payroll tax for their own retirement aligns with the early concept of social security and its arguments about the importance of linking "contributions" and benefits.

While most people think they are paying into their own retirement account, most people also favor transfers to the elderly.[11] This general commitment to care for the elderly explains the past political taboo on public discussions of social security. But few people understand fully the conflict between the program's insurance and transfer goals.

Combining retirement insurance and general support for the elderly, social security is intended both to replace a portion of a family's income after retirement (or after disability or death) and to assure a minimum income for the aged (or disabled and dependent survivors). The two objectives are very different, but both relate generally to the problem of security for the aged. In combination, however, they contribute to today's arguments about social security. The income replacement objective applies to all families. The welfare objective applies only to some individuals, regardless of taxes paid. Until now we have been able to accept both objectives under the vague rationales argued at social security's inception: that old people, the disabled, and dependent survivors should not be relegated to poverty and that the government should help protect wage earners from a loss of income after retirement.

Until recently little political pressure existed to clarify the conflict between social security's two goals. But the financial crisis has pushed the payroll tax close to its politically tolerable limit, and voters are beginning to understand the difficulties in trying to achieve income replacement and minimum income assurance through the same vehicle.

POLITICAL IMPLICATIONS

Over the years, social security has been described as an insurance program which links contributions and benefits, in order to encourage support for the system. In 1966 John Carroll of the Social Security Administration was rather surprisingly open about this when he wrote:

> It can scarcely be contested that earmarking of payroll taxes for OASDI reduced resistance to the imposition of taxes on low-income earners, made feasible tax increases at time(s) when they might not otherwise have been made, and has given trust fund programs a privileged position semi-detached from the remainder of government. Institutionalists foresaw these advantages as means to graft the new programs into the social fabric.[12]

This argument is a rather open deception. It may be found many times over in the social security literature: that workers have agreed to increased taxes because they expected a direct benefit.[13]

The perception of what people are paying and what they are receiving is critical in shaping their attitudes toward the program, and therefore in shaping political responses. In the past politicians and the Social Security Administration have encouraged the public to see only benefits, not costs. Increasing social security benefits involves explicit benefits; increasing payroll taxes involves the perception of negligible costs for most people, who think they are buying retirement insurance. Buying insurance, after all, does not reduce a person's wealth; it merely changes the *form of wealth,* substituting future for present benefit, like putting money in the bank.

Under the circumstances, apart from the ethics involved, it is not hard to see why policymakers have gone to such lengths to encourage people to think social security is a mechanism by which workers put away money for their future. Because people perceive payroll taxes as equivalent to insurance premiums, they believe that unlike all other public expenditures, social security spending is *free*—costless to taxpayers. The only perceived cost relates to the amount of future protection individual citizens want to buy for themselves, which varies from person to person. For those who want more protection, increasing the payroll tax will actually encourage the perception of *increased* benefit.

A related phenomenon exists with the employer contribution. While the burden of the employer contribution is largely if not entirely shifted to the employee, most employees see it as a payment by someone else to their retirement account. Again, they see no cost.

A program offering only benefits and no costs is of course a politician's dream. And that perception explains why throughout the history of social security, until only recently, political pressures pushed toward the transfer goal and away from insurance: transfers maximize "benefits" paid for by increasing "insurance premiums" that contributors expect to have returned. As the Carroll quotation above makes quite clear, in the past social security never had to compete with other social priorities. It was like a polit-ical joyride.

The Social Security Administration has a special stake in en-couraging and perpetuating the insurance myth, and especially in preserving social security's system of earmarked financing. As Aaron Wildavsky has noted, earmarked financing is the most secure kind of appropriation, and is therefore the ideal financing arrangement for any public bureaucracy. By protecting and de-fending the earned entitlement system paid for by earmarked fi-nancing, the Social Security Administration guarantees its own autonomy as a special, privileged preserve in official Washington.

Because past policy has rested on the public's misperception of social security, politicians are understandably reluctant to permit people to see the program as it really is. People will increase their payments far more willingly as "insurance premium" payers than as taxpayers. It is unlikely that people would tolerate the present payroll tax rates, especially the regressivity of the payroll tax, if they knew what the taxes were paying for. As long as people thought tax increases were going to benefit themselves directly, they were willing to support the increases, or at least not oppose them. If inflation, changing demographics, and increasing claims against the disability fund were not pushing upward the bill for the current arrangement, we could continue to fund it in a painless, and to many a seemingly equitable, manner. However, payroll taxes have now reached a point where it is no longer possible to increase benefits without political cost. Hence the political crisis.

The funding problem raises several important political questions. How long will voters agree to support increased payroll taxes? Will there be a demand to scale down benefits? What voter pressure will arise to reduce what many regard as income inequities?

The answers will depend, as they always have, on how people perceive the program. The funding crisis, especially as we approach the political limit to increases in the payroll tax, has reoriented the public perception of social security so that now, for the first time, the arguments for equity emphasize the insurance function: they attempt to relate what people pay in to what they will get back. Emphasizing the transfer goal, however, makes many "inequities" disappear.

The funding crisis and changing public perceptions of the program raise important opportunities for reform. While economists tell us what we *should* do, a more important question may be what *can* be done? In the realm of simple prediction, what *will* be done? Unfortunately, the prognosis is not encouraging. The long-term funding problem is predicted to become serious in the period after 2010 when the postwar baby boom reaches retirement age, and it is widely assumed this will present no serious political issue before that time. Since politicians operate on fairly short time horizons (rarely past the next election) the incentives are very strong for them to proceed with business as usual and let the "long term" problem correct itself in the long term. The most important of these incentives is that whatever one may think of its fairness, the payroll tax is a very efficient means of raising money. It exists and is in place. And for that reason no amount of prodding from economists or anybody else will convince Congress *voluntarily* to transfer any substantial part of social security to general revenues.

While major shifts to general revenue seem unlikely, smaller shifts may prove irresistible as the political limit of payroll tax increases is approached. Such limited shifts could have important effects on how social security is perceived; and since public perceptions are the key to the politics, even some general revenue funding could have a *major, potentially immediate* impact on political and social attitudes. Shifting perceptions could turn the "long term" problem into an immediate crisis—which current proposals before Congress are doing little to solve.

Substantively, the political and economic questions of assistance for the elderly are: How much of the national income do we wish to transfer? How much of other things do we want to give up to assist the aged? The question is not *whether,* but *how much.* It is a question which the past organization of social security funding, especially the myth that social security is retirement insurance, has obscured.

The discussion thus far should explain the considerable political pressures resisting any major disturbance to the present arrangement. This general conclusion should be evident in considering eight key proposals for change now being discussed.[14]

SHORT-RANGE PROPOSALS[15]

Increased Taxes

Social Security Commissioner James B. Cardwell follows the Social Security Administration's bureaucratic interest in earmarked financing by insisting that higher social security taxes are inevitable, if we are to pay the higher benefits scheduled for the future.[16] Among the organizations supporting increased taxes are business groups such as the U.S. Chamber of Commerce and the NAM, while the AFL-CIO, the National Council of Senior Citizens, and liberal Democrats oppose an increase because of its effect upon low- and middle-income workers.[17] Congressional critics argue that the payroll tax is regressive, due to this disproportionate burden. However, even opponents expect a tax increase. The question seems to be how large an increase, and what concessions might accompany one. Representative James Burke, Chairman of the Subcommittee on Social Security of the House Ways and Means Committee, a person who will play an important role in any compromise, would like to keep the tax rate under 6 percent for both the employee and the employer, so the maximum near-term increase might be .15 percent.[18]

Taxpayer reactions to the tax increase will tend to reflect their perceptions of its purpose. Opposition will be limited to increases for insurance, but the higher the payroll tax goes, the more it will lose its appearance as insurance premiums and the more it will look like general taxes. As more taxpayers recognize that social security taxes are not going into their personal reserve account, there will be pressure to make them do so. Social security now provides a mixed package of benefits—protection for dependent children and against disability during working years, as well as after-retirement income. Some portion of present payments, therefore, does represent insurance. The problem of evaluating its worth is compounded by uncertainty about how much redistribution Congress will enact in future years. But whatever the difficulty, all future benefits have a *present value* which varies for each taxpayer depending on attitudes and circumstances. Beyond that value, taxpayers can be expected to resist tax increases. The magnitude of the problem is indicated by Feldstein's calculation that an increase of 10 percentage points in the payroll tax could push some middle-income families' marginal tax rates close to 50 percent. [20]

Raise the Maximum Taxable Wage

This alternative method of increasing revenue is criticized because it might reduce savings and therefore capital formation. Further, to raise sufficient revenue the maximum may have to be increased greatly because of the smaller numbers of persons added as the level is increased. More important, this option would trigger larger benefits for the higher income persons affected by the higher wage base—persons who are already saving though private pensions and other investments. Nevertheless, the AFL-CIO favors this approach. Lawrence Smedley, associate director of the AFL-CIO's Social Security Department, argues that over the years the percentage of workers who have had all of their wages taxed has dropped from 97 percent to 85 percent.[21] The AFL-CIO recommends that the income ceiling be increased to $28,000 and that employers be taxed on their total payrolls, which would include the full salaries of highly paid corporate executives. The AFL-CIO also favors contributions from general revenues until at least one-third of the program is financed this way.[22]

Republicans and business oppose this alternative because they believe the wage base has already risen too rapidly, and they fear an increase in the wage base would trigger higher future benefits.

Another possibility is an increase in *both* the tax rate and the maximum taxable wage. Social Security Commissioner James Cardwell favors this compromise and gives as a reason his belief that dipping into general revenues would encourage increases in benefits.[23] But his position also reflects the agency's bureaucratic commitment to earmarked financing, which would be compromised perhaps irretrievably by payments from general revenue.

There is increasing pressure from many sides to do something, and increasing both the tax rate and the maximum taxable wage would be the easiest changes to make. The specific changes will almost certainly depend on the size of the expected deficit. As this chapter is being written, the Congressional Budget Office is suggesting a smaller near-term deficit than originally expected. If the deficit were small enough, it might be met by an increase in the wage base or by a small increase in the payroll tax rate. The shortfall depends upon the national economy and the extent of unemployment, and precise estimates are difficult to make. Other changes have been proposed that might be accepted in future years.

MID-RANGE PROPOSALS

Reduce Benefits

Former Treasury Secretary William Simon has argued that we will have to reduce the growth rate of social security benefits or face large and perhaps sudden cuts in benefits. He feels future taxpayers will not accept large tax increases passively, especially as they did not cause the problem.[24] Simon's proposals for cure include reducing the rate of benefit increases, increasing the retirement age, and taxing social security benefits.

Lowering social security benefits for those already receiving them is politically almost inconceivable, and reducing them for the increasing numbers of persons reaching retirement age is only slightly less so. Groups representing low-income and older people, notably the AFL-CIO, the National Retired Teachers Association, the American Association of Retired Persons, and the national Council of Senior Citizens, undertandably rejected the Hsaio panel recommendation, which would have reduced the income replacement ratio over the long run.[25]

Public expectations create a practical, political, and moral obligation to pay future benefits, which people feel they have earned. How much of an obligation is a question to be argued, but the answer must at least equal benefits taxpayers could have received in the private market. On average, current benefits are about three times the actuarial value of contributions. While it may be difficult to see a *moral* obligation to pay more than actuarial value, *political* pressures and precedents will almost certainly argue for more. But arguments for more may be overcome by the prospect of significant tax increases early in the next century, if not sooner.

Increase the Retirement Age

The age at which payments may be received could be raised, in effect reducing benefits. Secretary Simon suggested that it would be necessary to increase the retirement age gradually from 65 to 67 so as not to disrupt the plans of persons now nearing the retirement age. Similarly, the Wallis Social Security Advisory Council proposed that beginning in 2005 the age at which one could receive a partial pension be gradually moved from 62 to 68.[26]

The problem of changing the retirement age is made more difficult by the trend toward earlier rather than later retirement. Few people see this proposal being implemented in the near term, and major interest groups have not taken a position on it. Old-age interest groups may support an increased retirement age if this meant an increase rather than a reduction in benefits for those who remain in the work force beyond age 65. Further, these organizations may argue for a compromise, increasing both the retirement age and the earnings limit for retired persons.

Tax Social Security Income

This move would not affect the aged poor below the income tax threshold, and if the tax receipts were earmarked for the trust fund, this option would help reduce the shortfall. However, opposition would arise because of the fact that most people see social security as a self-purchased annuity.

Like proposals for reducing benefits and increasing the retirement age, the battle lines for this change are not drawn. Assuming traditional alliances, we should expect opposition from old-age interest groups and the majority in Congress.

LONG-TERM PROPOSALS

Alternatives to Social Security

The short-term deficits can be met by minor adjustments; the real problem will come after the turn of the century when the postwar baby boom retires. It is widely assumed that the tax levels necessary to pay the promises of social security could cause a taxpayers' revolt, but not until the financial crisis actually occurs. Thus *Forbes* has predicted that "long before payroll taxes hit 20 percent, the workingman will be in revolt against the lawmakers. Obviously, the politicians will soon be tapping general revenues rather than just payroll taxes. But how much more of a burden will the general taxpayer accept?"[27]

The extent of the funding problem is indicated by increasing municipal withdrawals. During the past several years well over 125 governmental units have pulled out of the program, and more than 200 others have stated their intention to do so.[28] If social security costs continue to grow, it is predicted that these pullouts will continue, although at present more government workers are entering than are withdrawing from the program.[29]

The funding problem forms one side of the political problem. The other side of the problem is that for most Americans social security is the major form of saving. They have paid into the program believing they have accumulated a contractual right to benefits. That expectation itself argues against radical changes in the present system, which despite its problems has accumulated moral, if not legal, obligations over its life. People still believe their taxes are being put away for them, and they are accustomed to seeing Congress raise benefits along with taxes. These expectations stand in the way of any major change in the program.

Place More Reliance on Private Pension Plans

Some observers such as Peter Drucker,[30] recognizing the growth of private pension plans, propose that social security be shifted as much as possible to private programs, leaving behind only the problem cases, those unable to be handled through a system based on actuarial principles. Social security would then be financed through general revenues, with contributing workers in the private system. The private system would be the primary source of insurance, as it soon will be anyway.

Increased reliance on private pensions will probably occur, especially as future social security benefits increase less quickly than they have in the past. The question is whether such reliance could (or should) occur by direct policy intervention, as recommended by some observers. In a 1974 article, for example, Roger LeRoy Miller proposed that social security be forced to make itself sound by issuing bonds from the Federal Reserve to cover the debt. This, he argued, would force Congress to act responsibly in that benefits could be increased only by issuing bonds to cover the new debt. People could also opt out of the system if they desired, as long as they could purchase a government-certified private annuity.[31]

These changes might occur. They may even improve the present system. Their fundamental defect, however, is that if any substantial number of people opt out, the reduced availability of funds to pay social security's current obligations would force a massive transfer of responsibility to the general fund. It is not at all clear that people would permit increased general taxes on a scale necessary to meet the new (potentially enormous) obligation.

Although sudden shifts to private pensions are extremely unlikely, a reduction in the growth rate of social security benefits will increase the relative importance of private pension income in the retirement security of the elderly.

FINANCE SOCIAL SECURITY
THROUGH GENERAL REVENUES

It is unlikely that any substantial part of the social security system will soon be financed through general revenues.[32] However, the anticipated short-run deficit might be financed through a one-time payment; Part A of Medicare (hospital insurance) might be switched from the payroll tax to general revenues; or payments to the aged poor beyond those due these persons from their social security taxes might be paid from general revenues.

The Wallis Advisory Council proposed using part of the present payroll tax earmarked for Medicare to pay for pensions, and funding the balance of Medicare from general revenues. Some members would even have general revenues pay for low-income pensions, at least that part which exceeds the wages received before retirement. However, the council did not recommend general revenue financing.[33]

Both President Ford and the 94th Congress opposed the idea of using general revenues to pay for any part of social security because this would make the program look less like a right earned by workers through their "contributions."[34] Former HEW Secretary Caspar Weinberger opposed the Advisory Council's suggestion to channel $7 billion to $8 billion of general tax revenues into Medicare because such a move would be "inappropriate for a program whose strength has depended so heavily on support by working people and their employers."[35] As noted, this position is also argued by spokesmen for the Social Security Administration, who seek to preserve the system of earmarked financing.

The major interest groups favoring general revenue financing include the AFL-CIO and old-age interest groups such as the National Council of Senior Citizens, the National Retired Teachers Association, and the American Association of Retired Persons. The AFL-CIO's Smedley gives the reason for their position by arguing that general revenue financing would make the system more equitable because income taxes are progressive.[36] Bills by Representative James Burke of Massachusetts and Senator Gaylord Nelson of Wisconsin address the regressiveness of the tax instruments.[37]

On the other hand, the NAM opposed general revenue funding, arguing that it would remove the visible profile of social security costs and would destroy the future stability of social security benefits.[38]

Both the groups in favor of general fund financing and those opposed to it may be taking odd positions in relation to their own self-interest. Business groups press for retaining the insurance aspect of social security while arguing for continued payroll taxes "in order to keep costs visible." But *it is precisely the insurance myth that makes costs born through the payroll tax invisible.* In the payroll tax, people see not costs but insurance premiums for which they will gain future benefits. Therefore, not only is the business perspective incorrect; anyone *really* concerned about costs would insist on transferring social security to the general fund, where taxes are perceived for what they are: actual costs.

Conversely, elderly groups, which presumably seek increased transfers, criticize the payroll tax. Will the elderly benefit by shifting the program to the general fund where real costs and tradeoffs become apparent? On the contrary. When social security benefits are perceived as costly, pressures to reduce them will be felt as never before.

Essentially the same concern should be felt by all people who support the transfer function and oppose the regressiveness of the payroll tax.[39] Shifting to the general fund, while it may eliminate some regressiveness, will draw attention to the full costs of the program and thereby squeeze the transfers.

In reviewing their positions on social security, it is interesting that political conservatives, generally committed to holding down government spending, may have encouraged increasing social security budgets by strict adherence to the payroll tax and the insurance myth. Political liberals, on the other hand, who generally favor increased public spending, are arguing a position which may *appear* to ease the problem of financing rising social security expenditures, but which could have exactly the opposite effect. The single group which has consistently argued a positon serving its own interest is the Social Security Administration.

Moving social security to general revenues will not necessarily mean an increase in funds for social security. As part of the general fund, social security will be in direct competition with other programs, and Congress will be forced to set budget priorities on welfare expenditures. New expenditures for social security might be financed by increased income taxes. However, for reasons already given, increasing earmarked payroll taxes and increasing general taxes are two very different things. It is particularly improbable that Congress would increase taxes directly when other, less politically costly solutions exist.

Increased expenditures for social security could be funded by debt, and by subsequent inflation. However, the past couple of years indicates that there are political limits to inflation, and we already may have surpassed them. More likely, funding social security benefits from general revenues would require cutbacks in other programs, or at least limitations in the rate at which they grow. Where the cuts would be made is anyone's guess, but competition would seem to come from other federal transfer programs, many of which already reach the elderly. Welfare expenditures and food stamps are two possibilities. Medicare and Medicaid are also significant areas, particularly if the talk about controlling the spiral in medical prices becomes policy in the form of price controls on physician fees and hospital costs. The experience in most other countries indicates that as health delivery is centralized, political pressure to limit expenditures tends to substitute resource-wasting forms of rationing, especially queuing, for rationing by price. Since queuing involves a cost that does not appear in national income accounts, it is politically very attractive. Most recent talk about national health insurance has stressed cost controls as a major benefit. By concealing the costs of national health insurance, resource-wasting forms of rationing would free general revenues to pay social security benefits.[40]

Lastly, the competition for federal funds might force reduction of such items as support for college students and social science research.

But there is a more fundamental problem with funding any part of social security from general revenues. It concerns public perceptions of the program. The great uncertainty in proposals to use general revenue is how such a move will affect the perceptions of individual employee-taxpayers toward social security as a program of earned entitlements. The problem is aggravated because any use of general revenues may become addictive, foreclosing a future possibility of return to the payroll tax. Such a change in perception could threaten the program's sense of equity and therefore its public support. This problem is particularly troublesome at a time, such as now, of rising public concern over the integrity of the earned entitlements, and especially of the concern that benefits be related to contributions.

Whatever the advisability of using general revenues, many people are still troubled with the regressivity of the payroll tax. One possible compromise might be to keep the payroll tax and add deductions or credits. The Tax Reduction Act of 1975 does this in part by introducing a 10 percent income tax credit on household earnings up to $4,000, phasing it out at higher levels. There is no reason why the Social Security Administration cannot live with this step toward a negative income tax, and even embrace it. Introducing progressivity into the payroll tax would reduce criticism of it, while maintaining the earmarked feature that bureaucrats have such an interest in preserving.

IMMINENT CHANGES

During his campaign President Carter made frequent promises to restore confidence in social security. This paper suggests, however, that Washington policymakers will lean over backward to do as little as possible, while trying to protect the fragile position of the trust fund. Many observers dismiss the trust fund as irrelevant to the broader questions of social security policy, but the trust fund does have in important mythical role in perpetuating public perception of social security as a system of earned entitlements. Were the trust fund to disappear entirely, a major change of perception could dramatically occur, and public support for social security could be fundamentally undermined. For that reason, we can expect that maintaining a trust fund of some credible size will remain a high priority for policymakers.

It is already clear that social security will take a back seat to almost every other conceivable priority of the House Ways and Means Committee, which would have to consider any important social security legislation. At present Mr. Carter's priorities for the committee include an economic stimulus package and tax reform, followed by energy measures, welfare reform, and national health insurance.[41] Those major issues will leave no time to consider serious social security legislation, and that is just how policymakers want it.

The Ways and Means Committee probably will have to do something about the short-term deficit, if only to protect the trust fund. What happens will depend largely on the economy. If the social security deficit is smaller than estimated, increasing the wage base might bring in enough money to solve the immediate problem without a tax increase.

To avoid increasing the wage base or the payroll tax, Congress might consider a one-time influx of general revenues to solve the short-term deficit. This has been suggested as a loan, but the program may not generate enough funds for repayment. Thus a one-time general revenue infusion may run into opposition as the forerunner of other payments from the general fund. More probable is a proposal for a modest tax increase now and a substantial one in the future, when times are better.

These competing proposals suggest a compromise such as an increase of .1 or .15 percent in the payroll tax boosted by an increase in the wage base to $17,700. In 1976 Representatives Ullman and Burke (chairmen, respectively, of the Ways and Means Committee and of the Ways and Means Social Security Subcommittee) supported a similar compromise. To this might be added a small payment from general revenues, with a tax increase when the economy has recovered. This compromise could solve social security's short-run problems without major political concessions. If Congress were not so concerned with preserving the trust funds, and time ran out, funds might be shifted from the retirement and survivor benefit fund (which is expected to be exhausted in the mid-1980s) to the disability fund, which will be depleted sooner (perhaps in 1979). But concern about the trust funds makes this doubtful.

CONCLUSION

Despite growing political support for some separation of social security functions, major funding with general revenues is years away. However, support for separation might increase if the public comes to see it as a means of making social security more equitable to individual contributors while meeting the commitment to social adequacy for the aged.

Strengthening the relationship between contributions and benefits, the insurance goal of social security, might permit Congress politically to separate the assistance/transfer program and finance it from general revenue. Strengthening the insurance purpose would also make workers more inclined to accept increases in the payroll tax. In the long run, if assistance to the poor could be accomplished through a modified SSI program, social security benefits could be related directly to contributions.

It seems probable that eventuallly we would have a formalized three-tier program. The means test program, financed from general revenues, will be offered in the modified SSI program or its successor—perhaps a negative income tax. The second component will be the social security insurance program based on payroll taxes. And the third component will be private pensions, personal savings, and other sources of revenue to provide additional income during retirement. This three-tier system would be further augmented, and the insurance goal strengthened, by eliminating the earnings retirement test, which would permit the elderly to supplement their income by working.

A three-tier system will evolve only if the present structure maintains enough public confidence to permit gradual reform. A sudden crisis of confidence would make all predictions impossible. Unfortunately, the present patterns of official thinking may produce just such a crisis, particularly since most policymakers assume the long-term funding problem can be left to be solved in the long term. A clear understanding of the problem, and especially of the perceptions that underlie the program's past public support, will dramatize the need for immediate action to avoid a crisis that may be difficult to contain.

Public support for social security has always depended on a clear understanding of the program as an insurance system of earned entitlements, in which workers put away funds for their own future. The perception of the payroll tax as personal savings has encouraged both politicians and the public to see only benefits in social security, not costs. However, this "free" arrangement has depended on an expanding economy to keep it going. Recent demographic changes have therefore threatened the very basis of the system.

If past conditions have allowed only benefits to be seen, the real future danger is that in changing conditions the situation may be reversed and people may begin to see only costs and liabilities. It could happen on both the tax side and the benefit side: rising payroll taxes (or a shift to general revenues) could erode the public's perception of the earmarked payroll tax; and the resulting taxpayer resistance to further increases (or even demands that taxes be reduced) would put pressure on the benefit side, forcing the prospect of benefit reductions.

The dangers in current public discussion of social security result from a tendency to see the program as merely a projection of the past. This tendency encourages those concerned only with the present and the near future, including most policymakers, to do nothing about what they see as a distant problem. This is a serious mistake. Changing public perceptions of the program will threaten the foundations of public support for it, and those changes can only be accelerated by the funding crisis.

The situation implies that the "long-term problem" may have a much shorter fuse than most people, including most politicians, realize. The long-term funding crisis will not become acute when its direct financial consequences are felt early in the next century. It will become acute when the current working generation perceives correctly the nature of the taxes they are paying, and when they realize the present costs they are bearing on behalf of a very much leaner future. The great political crisis will not hit when the future arrives. It will be upon us the moment future expectations exert a strong force on present behavior.

For most of its history social security seemed to offer nothing but benefits for politicians and public alike. Unfortunately, the future may bring just the opposite: a nightmare combination of declining benefits and rising taxpayer resistance to a program that is not what they thought it was. Farsighted policymakers should feel immediate urgency about correcting a long-term problem. But declining demographics make real solutions hard to come by. And without "real solutions" most policymakers will be inclined to do nothing until the crisis actually occurs.

Doing nothing may turn out to be politically and socially the most damaging action of all.

IX

MICHAEL J. BOSKIN

SOCIAL SECURITY: THE ALTERNATIVES BEFORE US

History and goals. Changes in the economy. Lengthening retirement. Changing demographics. Problems with social security. Double index-ing for inflation. Inequities. Is social security regressive overall? The effect on capital formation and on labor force participation. The long-term deficit. Toward a solution. Separating the insurance and transfer components. Transfers to the non-poor. Financing transfers from general revenue. Separate social insurance. Problems with pay-as-you-go financing. Minimum income support for the aged. Toward a genuine trust fund.

Since its enactment in 1935, the social security system has enjoyed unique popularity among public income support programs. In the past several years, however, rising payroll taxes, a huge long-term deficit, and doubts about its effect on the overall economy has led an increasing number of observers to conclude that social security is in urgent need of reform.

173

BACKGROUND

Social security was enacted during the Great Depression. In four decades, coverage has been extended, taxes and benefits increased, and other modifications made; but during that time the system's essential features have remained unchanged. Workers pay contributions—which are really taxes—and receive benefits, partly dependent on past taxes. The nature and relationship of taxes and benefits reveal the basic nature of the program.

Taxes are levied at a flat rate on both employees and employers on all covered earnings up to a current maximum ceiling of $16,500. There are no exemptions or deductions. While the employer nominally pays one-half of the tax, Break notes that economists generally agree that the employee bears this burden in the form of lower wages. Computing total employee contributions, therefore, requires combining the total of employer and employee contributions.

Although benefits paid to beneficiaries depend partly on past earnings and increase as past earnings increase, they do so in less than direct proportion. The benefits formula is thus weighted toward low-income workers. Also, benefits are paid on a family basis, while taxes are levied on individuals.

Finally, and in some ways most important, the system is financed on a pay-as-you-go basis, whereby current payroll taxes are used to pay current benefits. The "contributions" are not invested as are private insurance premiums. There is no real capital accumulation, and no real interest accrues. The taxpayer is financing a government program—retirement benefits for the elderly—not, as most people think, saving for his or her own retirement in any direct sense. Benefits for the current working generation must come from taxes paid by the next working generation.

This system serves two major goals: to replace income lost at retirement, and to provide minimum income support for the aged. The former, the insurance goal, is based on earned entitlements; the welfare or transfer goal aims at social adequacy of support. Each goal enjoys wide public support as well as important policy justifications. Viscusi and Zeckhauser discuss imperfections in the private annuities market as one set of problems. In addition, imperfect foresight regarding future incomes, inflation, life expectancy, etc., may lead many citizens to "undersave" for retirement, forcing them as general charges on the public via welfare or other programs.

Over the last four decades, the social security system has helped mitigate these problems in an important way. It has provided substantial income security to the elderly; it has kept many elderly persons out of extreme poverty; and it has transferred billions of dollars annually from the younger, wealthier generation of workers to the older, poorer generation of retirees. These are significant achievements indeed. However, the system, which was designed decades ago, has not kept up fully with rapidly changing economic, social, and demographic conditions. It is having several substantial and probably unintended adverse effects on the overall economy; and it faces a long-term funding crisis of immense proportions. In addressing the problem of reform, it is important that we build on the program's achievements while ameliorating its harmful effects on the economy and improving the prospects for its long-term viability.

SOCIAL SECURITY AND THE ECONOMY

Since the enactment of social security in 1935, dramatic changes have occurred in the U.S. economy. Among the most important are the continual growth of real per capita income; a rapid general growth of government, especially in income security programs; a sharp increase in the labor force participation of married women; an increase in martital instability; a trend toward earlier retirement; an increase in the life expectancy of the elderly; an equalization of the income distribution; an enormous growth of private pensions; and a sharp decline in the birthrate. Each of these changes has important consequences for social security.

The trend to earlier retirement combined with increased life expectancy.has increased markedly the average time between retirement and death. When social security was enacted, half of all males over 65 were in the labor force. Today the figure is only one in five.

More persons now receive their first social security benefits at age 62 than at 65. Average life expectancy of 60-year-olds has increased about two years. The average length of retirement has thus increased by about one-third over the 1935 level. This substantial lengthening has greatly strained the financial resources of the elderly. To achieve the same real level of consumption per year during retirement, a retiree now needs substantially greater savings, or intrafamily transfers, or public support.

Social security itself is partly responsible for the sharp decline in the labor force participation of the elderly. Elsewhere I have estimated that about two-thirds of the decline is due to the increase in social security benefits and to the earnings test (which reduces benefits when earnings exceed a modest amount).[1]

One might expect that a large increase in the length of retirement would normally lead to increased saving. But the saving rate in the U.S. over this period has actually declined slightly,[2] for two principal reasons. First, sharply increased taxation of income from capital has drastically reduced the real net return on saving, which in turn has depressed saving substantially.[3] Second, the expectation of social security benefits to finance retirement consumption has probably reduced private saving for retirement.

Earlier retirement and greater life expectancy imply a longer period of retirement. At the same time, the rapid expansion of college enrollment has increased the average pre-work years. Thus total years of employment have declined significantly. Even with a stable age structure in the population, these twin features of our economy will alter patterns of intrafamily economic dependency and cooperation.

Perhaps even more important than the increased life expectancy and earlier retirement is the dramatic change in the age structure of the population. The post-World War II baby boom has given way to a sharp decrease in the birthrate below both historical averages and the replacement rate. While it is difficult to forecast fertility behavior into the distant future, unless a sharp increase in the birthrate occurs, the population as a whole will continue to grow older. This will leave us with the awkward prospect of a huge increase in the ratio of retired persons to workers when the baby boom generation begins to retire around the year 2010. The best estimate is that the ratio of retirees to workers will increase by about 50 percent—from slightly less than one in three to about one in two. Given the pay-as-you-go nature of the system, this implies either a huge increase in taxes to maintain the ratio of benefits to wages or a significant decline in the ratio. Neither prospect is appealing, but there is no avoiding the choice.

Unanticipated inflation destroys the real value of assets and strikes the elderly more severely than the general population. Historically, social security benefits were adjusted periodically by Congress. They are now indexed automatically to account for general price level increase. Unfortunately, a technical mistake in the indexing technique overadjusts for inflation and, if left uncorrected, doubles the system's enormous projected long-run deficit.[4]

Finally, the growth of private pension plans—partly in response to tax incentives—has created an alternative source of retirement income for the elderly. The availability of private pensions and annuities has important consequences for the design of social security.

These factors reveal the interaction and mutual effects of social security and the general economy, effects which are important in considering some of the major problems with social security as currently organized.

PROBLEMS WITH SOCIAL SECURITY

Besides short-run structural problems such as the overindexing for inflation, several long-run problems with social security have emerged in recent years. These include issues of equity, adverse incentives, and stupendous long-run deficits.

The relationship between taxes paid and benefits received is far from perfect for at least two reasons. First, a large proportion of benefits is really an intergenerational transfer. Second, as Campbell argues in Chapter VII, different groups in the population are treated differently. Lower-income workers receive a lower fraction of their previous earnings in benefits than do high-income workers; married couples usually receive half again as much as single persons with the same earnings history for the primary earner, etc. These perceived inequities among groups revolve around the failure to tie benefits directly to taxes paid plus interest.

Social security has also been criticized for levying a regressive tax on payrolls. A flat-rate tax on payrolls is regressive because labor income (earnings) goes largely to low- and middle-income workers. The problem is aggravated by the fact that employees ultimately pay both parts of the tax, and by the ceiling on taxable earnings. This problem has led Pechman and others to propose general revenue financing of at least part of social security.

There are at least two problems with arguments about the regressivity of the payroll tax. First, it is not necessary to require every dollar of government revenue to be raised from progressive tax sources. The overall government impact on income distribution is important; the particular effect of one component is not. However, the rapid growth of social security benefits and hence payroll taxes—each is now the second largest and most rapidly growing item on their respective sides of the federal budget—has reduced the overall progressivity of federal taxation.

Second, it is not only taxes that are important, but the overall progressivity of the social security taxes *and* benefits. Overall, social security benefits are extremely progressive. Parsons and Munro demonstrate thay they consist largely (though at a declining rate) of transfers from a younger working generation to an older retired generation. Real per capita income in the U.S. has grown an average of about 2.5 percent per year. In the twenty-five years between generations, real incomes per capita approximately double. Thus social security transfers billions of dollars from a generation which on average is twice as wealthy as its parents to those parents. The benefit formula also contains a tilt in favor of low-income workers. Overall, the social security system has been extremely progressive.

The argument about the effect of social security taxes and benefits on overall income distributions also ignores the system's potential effects on labor supply and capital accumulation. As Feldstein and Rosen argue above, social security may retard capital formation. If so, it has reduced available capital per worker in the economy. Just as a farmer is more productive with a tractor than a shovel, workers in general are more productive with more capital per worker. Since productivity is the primary determinant of wage rates in the economy, social security may have reduced wage rates (and increased the rate of return on a smaller capital stock). This effect mitigates somewhat the overall progressivity of the system.

The adverse incentives created by the social security system on capital formation and retirement decisions are extremely important in their own right. As Feldstein notes,[5] any reduction in saving induced by the pay-as-you-go nature of social security implies a reduction in national income. Rosen argues that the implicit return in social security is quite low—approximately the sum of the growth of population (about 1 percent per year) and real wages (about 2.5 percent), or just under 4 percent; the social return on private saving is perhaps twice as large by my estimate, on the order of 10 percent.

Any decrease in private saving for retirement obviously subverts a major goal of social security: to provide retirement income. The same is true of the large effect of social security on earlier retirement. These adverse incentives combine to make the net impact of social security on the retirement income of the elderly substantially less than the total benefits paid.

Probably the most overwhelming problem confronting social security as a pay-as-you-go system is the long-term funding crisis. Even after correcting for the overindexing of benefits for inflation, a long-term deficit of approximately $1.1 trillion remains.[6] This is the amount by which the present value of legislated benefits exceeds the present value of legislated taxes. To put this in perspective, this amount is approximately twice the size of the national debt, and more than a decade's worth of social security taxes at present rates.

The major cause of this projected deficit is the drastic change in the age structure of the population. Once the post-World War II baby boom retires—around 2010—the ratio of retirees to workers will increase enormously. If birthrates fail to increase substantially, a relatively small cohort of workers will be faced with large increases in social security taxes to finance benefits for a relatively large cohort of retirees. While this new generation of workers will be spending comparatively less in public support of the young for education, welfare, etc., the latter programs are heavily financed at the state and local levels of government and have their own favored interest groups to resist expenditure reductions. And even sharply reduced spending on public programs affecting the young will make little dent in the huge projected social security deficit, though part of the slack may be taken up by increased wages of the relatively scarce younger workers.

Beyond its consequences for social security, the changing age structure of the population has profound psychological and sociological implications. Not only will the population be aging, but in one generation the population will experience a massive shift from a large proportion of dependent children to a large proportion of quasi-dependent parents.

These three related sets of problems plague social security: inequities, adverse incentives, and long-run deficits. Several policy options exist for dealing with them.

TOWARD A SOLUTION

The social security system is widely heralded—and rightly so—by the public as a vital element in our income security system. Yet its essential features were designed under the very different economic and social conditions of four decades ago. Today social security is badly in need of reform, in part because of changing economic conditions and the development of other public and private programs, and in part because of the impending financial crisis caused by drastic changes in the age structure of the population.

The three sets of problems plaguing social security—the long-term funding deficit, the apparent inequities, and the adverse incentives—fortunately have a common solution: the separation of the transfer and annuity goals of the program, and the building of a trust fund to finance the insurance component while financing the transfers out of general revenues.[7]

The social security funding crisis is the dominant concern of policymakers and the public alike. It is a major cause of both rising payroll taxes and of most concerns about fairness. It must therefore be a central issue of reform.

For reasons given by Parsons and Munro and by Patton, solving the long-term funding problem cannot be left to the long term. It must become an immediate priority for policymakers, since the very basis of public support for the program depends on confidence in its solvency. Without serious reform, severe political and economic problems could soon occur. Those who think we have decades to solve the problem have misunderstood it.

In addressing the long-term problem, there are two major objectives for policy: first, to strengthen confidence in the program as an earned benefits, insurance program; and second, to reduce the gap between obligations and taxes. The latter can be accomplished either by increased revenues, reduced benefits, or both. These two objectives can be addressed precisely by separating the two goals of social security, funding the insurance part from a separate program, and gradually shifting transfer responsibilities to general revenues.

Separating the Transfer and Insurance Components

Many problems in the social security system relate to the conflict between its twin goals of earned benefits and income adequacy. Most critics of the program propose reforming it in the direction of one goal or the other.

Under the present system about two-thirds of current benefits represent intergenerational transfers, although this percentage will decline over time. Benefits are also weighted in favor of lower-income recipients. One major problem in recommending reforms involves defining the transfer or welfare goal. The central question is whether we have a genuine social interest in transferring income from the present generation of taxpayers to current retirees who are not poor and would not be poor in the absence of social security. If not, separating the transfer and insurance goals of the program presents no problem: a separate insurance program could return contributions plus accrued interest; and transfers based on need could be paid from general revenues. Continuing the intergenerational transfer without regard to need increases the taxes necessary to finance the benefits, while reducing the incentive to make difficult judgments about need.

Evaluating need involves a tough empirical question about the status of the elderly without social security. The answer to this question depends on several issues raised above: Does social security substitute for private savings for retirement? Does it induce earlier retirement? Does it replace private intrafamily transfers of income? Enough empirical evidence has accumulated to suggest that the net impact of social security on the retirement income of the elderly is substantially less than the actual benefits paid. However, a large percentage of the elderly population relies quite heavily on social security benefits and a nontrivial percentage would probably be destitute in the absence of the program. It is hard to say how many "free riders" would fail to save for their own future because of the program.

The current system might seem to indicate broad public support for assistance to the elderly non-poor; but given current legislation, this element is declining. Moreover, it is difficult to separate present assistance patterns from the start-up phase of the program, when there was general agreement to include poor and non-poor alike. Perhaps most important of all, evaluations of public support for assistance to the non-poor are only as valid as public awareness both of the extent of that assistance and of its costs. Friedman notes that the mythologies of the "employer contribution" and "trust fund" cast extreme doubt on public awareness of full benefits and costs.

It is difficult to forecast whether or not the intergenerational transfer will continue to decline, or whether current workers will get a favorable break from the next generation. Part of the answer depends on the future growth of income and population; and although current population trends are not promising in this regard, reliable forecasting is extremely difficult.

We thus have several possible systems and combinations of systems: pure (poverty only) transfer, pure insurance, mixed transfer (poverty plus earnings-related benefits above poverty levels), and combinations. In a growing economy, the willingness of successive generations to provide for the elderly is likely to change over time, as are the basic need standards.

In principle, it is desirable to separate the financing of these different goals of the system—insurance, minimum support, and earnings cushion beyond poverty. As noted, the last of these is uncertain, given its historical decline; but it probably still accounts for a substantial component of current benefits.

Transfers to the elderly poor should be financed from general revenues. It makes little sense to finance an income guarantee for the aged poor from a tax which bears so heavily on the working poor.[8] The current income tax exemptions, deductions, and low-income allowance, which together exempt the first several thousand dollars of earnings from tax, indicate the general belief that those at the very bottom of the income scale should not have to help finance general expenditures. (Break and Pechman note, however, that the earned income credit refunds part of social security taxes to very low-income workers.)

The same argument applies to any intergenerational transfers providing earnings-related benefits beyond those provided by pure insurance and the minimum income guarantee. It makes little sense for current unskilled workers to surrender income (beyond their *own* insurance) to subsidize retired doctors and lawyers beyond actuarially sound returns.

In separating the insurance from the transfer goals, general revenue financing will also require the transfer goals to compete openly with other government priorities, including tax cuts. As Patton argues, a major problem with earmarked funding of transfer payments is that the public is prevented from clearly seeing costs and benefits. General revenue financing will permit policymakers and the public openly to determine the value of transfers to the elderly in relation to other social priorities.

Finally, there is the case for compulsory insurance. However society wishes to help the aged poor, the problem remains of preventing those who can provide for themslves from relying on transfers from society at large. By requiring insurance purchases providing at least poverty-level income, moderate-income workers would be prevented from opting out of the system during their working lives and then receiving the minimum guarantee upon retirement. This is the most telling argument for compulsory insurance.

These general principles suggest possible policy options.

Social Insurance. The compulsory insurance component of social security could be improved by increasing the scope of choice open to workers. There is no sound reason, for instance, that evidence of private insurance cannot eventually be used to satisfy the requirement of providing for personal retirement.

A reasonable system would require everyone to use a certain percentage of income or earnings to purchase social security or private pensions. The only remaining question is whether we should require insurance above the minimum for people who can afford it.

Workers should not be limited in their purchases of social security any more than they are limited in their purchases of private insurance. We want to encourage purchases wherever they are most efficient.

Separating the insurance component of social security will greatly strengthen the relationship between contributions and benefits and thereby greatly strengthen general confidence in the program. As Patton argues, without a clear determination to separate program goals, the use of general revenues may threaten public support for social security in a fundamental way. Clearly separating the insurance and transfer goals will avoid that problem.

Creating a strong insurance program will also mitigate problems currently felt with the retirement earnings test. Since benefits will be earned, no earnings test would apply to the insurance part.

The question remains about the funding structure for the separate insurance program—whether it should continue as a pay-as-you-go system, or whether a genuine effort should be made to accumulate a real trust fund.

Ideally, social insurance as insurance should not be financed on a pay-as-you-go basis, except in the historically unimportant case where economic growth rates exceed the rate of interest. Ideally, a separate insurance fund should be accumulated and invested in productive economic activity; in analogy with private insurance, the fund should be actuarially sound. However, the original design of social security has not followed this pattern, and because of implicit claims and explicit expectations that have developed, any sudden movement to full funding would be undesirable. A gradual movement in this direction, however, would be desirable for several reasons I shall discuss presently.

Minimum Income Support for the Aged. Minimum income support can be achieved either directly or by integration with a comprehensive income maintenance plan such as a negative income tax. In an integrated system, assistance could be augmented by special credits for the elderly, just as the income tax now allows them an extra exemption.

In the meantime, the new Supplemental Security Income program should be expanded to general revenue financing of full minimum income support. This would ease the burden on low-income payroll workers.

Such a system could easily be integrated into a negative income tax at a later date by allowing current retirees under social security to choose when to switch into the new program.

The switch from payroll to income tax financing of the transfer goals could be done directly, by nominal rate changes, or by integrating this part of the payroll tax with the income tax. The latter could be accomplished by allowing a credit against income tax payments with reimbursement for overpayments (which would not be infrequent) refunded through the income tax. This would provide a minimum *overall* exemption from taxation. A partial step in this direction would be to adopt a system of minimum exemptions and deductions in the payroll tax itself.

A Genuine Trust Fund

Gradually building a genuine social security trust fund to finance the insurance component would help solve three major problems associated with the program's current structure. First, it would eliminate inequities stemming from a perceived discrepancy between taxes paid and benefits received. Groups deserving special treatment could be dealt with in explicit transfer programs financed from general revenues.

Second, as Feldstein has emphasized, a social security fund is a way of dealing with any adverse incentives in capital accumulation.[9]

Finally, and perhaps most important, the trust fund would be accruing revenues and interest to provide flexibility in dealing with the impending, immense deficit caused largely by demographic changes in the population. If the actuarially sound trust fund approach were later deemed unwarranted on its own merits, both principal and accrued interest could be used to finance the impending increase in benefit entitlements.

Gradually building a trust fund will begin to deal with each of these problems, while leaving us several options later in the century for solving them. If we do not begin now, our options will be severely limited as we approach a major economic and political crisis.

We must begin to deal with these problems soon, or see the already adverse consequences worsen in the years ahead. The best place to start is with the separation of the transfer and insurance goals of the system and the gradual building of a genuine social insurance system.

APPENDICES

IV. Donald Parsons and Douglas R. Munro, "Intergenerational Transfers in Social Security"

The Methodology of the Welfare Component Calculation

The calculation of present values of taxes paid and benefits received by retirement cohort requires a number of assumptions, the most important of which include:

(1) The cohort contributes continuously from 1 January 1937 until age 65, at which time cohort members retire.

(2) The cohort pays an average tax per member in each year.

(3) The Old Age and Survivors Insurance portion of total social security contributions, reduced 20 percent to adjust for the survivors program, is the appropriate retirement contribution.

(4) Both the employee and employer contribution are attributed to the employee (otherwise the earned proportion is reduced by one-half).

(5) Members of the cohort have mortality expectations comparable to the male population as a whole at that age.

(6) The relevant interest rate is the nominal rate on short-term commercial paper.

VII. Rita Ricardo Campbell, "The Problems of Fairness"

The Homemaker

None of the several advisory groups to the Executive Branch and to Congress found an acceptable solution to estimate imputed homemaker income as a basis for social security taxes and future benefits. Attempts to solve the problem usually create new inequities, as claimed by individuals employed part time and performing similar duties, or by others who work for pay full time and also perform similar or allied "homemaker" duties, such as gardening. To estimate imputed income for one purpose would not, moreover, automatically exempt that income from personal income taxes. If the major aim of the social security system is to replace lost earnings, it is important to point out that in a technical sense there are no "earnings" for the homemakes to lose. This in no way denies that homemakers make a considerable contribution to society, but rather that society has failed to recognize this in its monetary accounting systems. Reforming social security, however, is not the best method for correcting this more fundamental problem.

REFERENCES

III. W. Kip Viscusi and Richard Zeckhauser
"The Role of Social Security in Income Maintenance"

Aaron, Henry. 1974. Demographic Effects on the Equity of Social Security Benefits. University of Maryland, processed.

Beier, Emerson. 1971. Incidence of Private Pension Plans. *Monthly Labor Review* 94, July.

Bixby, Lenore. 1970. Income of People Aged 65 and Over: Overview from 1968 Survey of the Aged. *Social Security Bulletin* 33, April.

Boskin, Michael. 1977. Social Security and Retirement Decisions. *Economic Inquiry* , January.

Brittain, John. 1972. *The Payroll Tax for Social Security.* Washington, D.C.: Brookings Institution.

Brown, J. Douglas. 1972. *An American Philosophy of Social Security: Evolution and Issues.* Princeton: Princeton University Press.

Feldstein, Martin. 1974. Social Security, Induced Retirement, and Aggregate Capital Accumulation. *Journal of Political Economy*

Friedman, Milton. 1962. *Capitalism and Freedom.* Chicago: University of Chicago Press.

Henle, Peter. 1972. Recent Trends in Retirement Benefits Related to Earnings. Reprint 241. Washington, D..C.: Brookings Institution.

Pechman, Joseph, Aaron, Henry, and Taussig, Michael. 1968. *Socal Security: Perspectives for Reform.* Washington, D.C.: Brookings Institution.

Shepard, Donald. 1977. Utility of Reducing the Probability of Death as a Function of Age: Results Derived from a Utility Function on Consumption. Boston: Havard School of Public Health.

U.S. Bureau of the Census. 1972a. Census of Population 1970. *General Population Characteristics.* Final Report PC(1)-B1, U.S. Summary. Washington, D.C.: U.S. Government Printing Office.

.1972b. Illustrative Population Projections in the United States: The Demographic Effects of Alternative Paths to Zero Growth. *Current Population Reports.* Series P-25, no. 480. Washington, D.C.: U.S. Government Printing Office.

.1972c. Projections of the Population of the United States by Age and Sex: 1972 to 2000. *Current Population Report.* Series P-25, no. 493. Washington, D.C.: U.S. Government Printing Office.

.1973. Census of Population 1970. *Employment Status and Work Experience.* Washington, D.C.: U.S. Government Printing Office.

U.S. Bureau of Labor Statistics. Selected issues, n.d. *Employment and Earnings.* Washington, D.C.: U.S. Government Printing Office.

U.S. Social Security Administration. Selected issues, n.d. *Social Security Bulletin.* Washington, D.C.: U.S. Government Printing Office.

Viscusi, W. Kip, and Zeckhauser, Richard. Forthcoming. *Welfare of the Elderly.* New York: Wiley-Interscience. Summarized in Discussion Paper 25D, Kennedy School of Government, Harvard University, October 1974.

NOTES

I. Edward Cowan: "Background and History: The Crisis in Public Finance and Social Security"

1. "Social Security in Review," *Social Security Bulletin* 40 (January 1977):1.

2. "Commissioner's Briefing Notes in 1976 Trustees Reports," in Social Security Administration, *Public Information Program Circular,* no. 217, 24 May 1976, p.2.

3. U.S. Congress, House, Committee on Ways and Means, *1976 Annual Report of the Board of Trustees of the Federal Old-Age and Survivors Insurance and Disability Insurance Trust Funds,* 94th Congress, 2d Session, 25 May 1976, p. 24. The estimate of $34.3 billion occurs for all three sets of economic assumptions.

4. Frances Perkins, *The Roosevelt I Knew* (New York, 1946), pp. 287, 293.

5. *Trustees Report,* pp.1-2.

6. Ibid., p.2.

7. Ibid., p.3.

8. A. Hasworth Robertson, "The Cost of Social Security: 1976-2050," speech (mimeo), Social Security Administration, Baltimore (n.d.), p. 5.

9. Ibid., p. 6.

10. Alicia Munnell, *The Future of Social Security (Washington D.C.,* in press). p. 32.

11. Robertson, "The Cost of Social Security," p. 7.

12. U. S. Congress, House, Committee on Ways and Means, Senate, Committee on Finance, *Report of the Consultant Panel on Social Security to the Congressional Research Service,* 94th Congress, 2d Session, August 1976, p. 3.

13. *Trustees Report,* p. 4.

14. *Wall Street Journal,* 21 December 1976.

15. Interview, 2 February 1977.

II A. Martin Feldstein: "Social Security"

1. These desired reforms are discussed in Martin Feldstein, "Facing the Social Security Crisis," *The Public Interest* (Spring 1977), and in idem., "Social Security Benefits and Financing," *American Economic Review* (forthcoming).

2. Idem., "Social Security, Induced Retirement and Aggregate Capital Accumulation," *Journal of Political Economy* (1974).

3. This social security "wealth" is not real wealth but only an implicit promise that the next generation will tax itself to pay the annuities currently specified in the law. Although there are

no tangible assets corresponding to this "wealth," it is perfectly rational for households to regard the value of their future social security benefits as part of their personal wealth.

4. A review of these studies is presented in Martin Feldstein, "Social Security and Savings: The Extended Life-Cycle Theory," *American Economic Review*, Proceedings, May 1976.

5. The idea of a social security fund is developed in idem., "Toward a Reform of Social Security," *The Public Interest* (Summer 1975); estimates of the consequences of such a fund are presented in idem., "The Social Security Fund and National Capital Accumulation," in *Funding Pensions: The Issues and Implications for Financial Markets* (Federal Reserve Bank of Boston, 1977).

IIB. Milton Friedman: "Payroll Taxes, No; General Revenues, Yes"

1. In writing this, I have used large parts of my column, "Truth in Advertising," *Newsweek*, 14 June 1971.

2. *Your Social Security*, HEW Publication No. (SSA) 76-10035, June 1976.

3. See especially, Milton Friedman and Wilbur Cohen, *Social Security: Universal or Selective?* (Washington, D.C., 1972).

III. W. Kip Viscusi and Richard Zeckhauser: "The Role of Social Security in Income Maintenance"

1. For an articulate statement of the conservative position on this issue, see Friedman (1962).

2. Two treatments of social security that criticize the program's distributional implications are the studies by Brittain (1972) and Pechman, Aaron, and Taussig (1968). See also article by Friedman in this volume.

3. These figures are from the *Social Security Bulletin* 39, no. 11 (March 1976):62.

4. See Henle (1972).

5. Brittain (1972) provides a detailed analysis of the payroll tax and its implicit rate of return.

6. In New York State in FY 1976, Medicaid spent $224 monthly per recipient. Comparable per recipient monthly figures were $111 for AFDC, $144 for SSI, $17 for food stamps, and $117 for general relief. Nationwide, two-thirds of total federal welfare expenditures are for Medicaid. See *New York Times*, 9 January 1977.

7. See Viscusi and Zeckhauser (forthcoming) for data sources and more precise budgetary breakdowns.

8. Unfortunately, administrative inadequacies in the SSI program have tarnished the impressive record of the Social Security Administration. A recent GAO study showed that in its first two years of existence SSI made overpayments of $1 billion. See *New York Times*, 21 November 1976.

9. Brown (1972) provides a very detailed discussion of the origins and motivations behind the Social Security Act.

10. Both Brittain (1972) and Pechman, Aaron, and Taussig (1973) advocate reforms of this type. It should be noted that the introduction of the SSI program had made the Social Security Administration's total operations more progressive.

11. The data below exclude the value of in-kind transfers which, as we saw earlier, was not particularly great.

12. All data discussed below are from the 1970 U.S. Census. In particular, See U.S. Bureau of the Census (1972a).

13. Shepard (1976) has computed optimal savings and consumption patterns for an individual with a typical lifetime earnings profile, no access to annuities, and only the knowledge that he would be subject to observed mortality rates. The period utility function is consumption raised to the .2 power; the discount rate is .05. Optimal consumption declines rapidly, since the desire not to die with assets on hand distorts the ideal pattern of level consumption.

14. See U.S. Bureau of Labor Statistics, *Employment and Earnings* 20, no. 1 (July 1973):58.

15. This drop is not surprising, given that a major objective of social security was to remove elderly individuals from the labor force so that younger people could take their places.

16. See Viscusi and Zeckhauser (forthcoming). The relation between work effort and benefits clearly goes in both directions, since reduced work by the elderly leads to higher benefit levels, which result from reduction of the earnings penalty amount. If some unobserved factor led to a decline in labor force participation and if average benefits for new "retirees" were greater than for existing recipients, then higher benefits would also correlate with decreases in participation. We cannot get the precise information we would like on this matter, since historically the marginal penalty rate on earnings has not varied.

17. Proposals to remove the earning test are frequently made in Congress. A present one is sponsored by Senator Durkin (D., N.H.).

18. See U.S. Bureau of the Census (1972c).

19. See U.S. Bureau of the Census (1972b). The fact that social security is not funded in advance but rather on a pay-as-you-go basis may delay such a revolt until the crisis in social security is imminent.

20. For a fuller articulation of our policy proposals, see Viscusi and Zeckhauser (forthcoming).

IV. Donald Parsons and Douglas R. Munro: "Intergenerational Transfers in Social Security"

1. James Buchanan, "Social Insurance in a Growing Economy: A Proposal for Radical Reform," *National Tax Journal* 21 (1968): 386-95; Colin Campbell, "Social Insurance in the United States: A Program in Search of an Explanation," *Journal of Law and Economics* 12 (1969): 249-65.

2. Henry Aaron, "Benefits under the American Social Security System," in Otto Eckstein, ed., *Studies in the Economics of Income Maintenance* (Washington, D.C., 1967), pp. 49-72; Joseph Pechman et al., *Social Security: Perspectives for Reform* (Washington, D.C., 1968), chapter 9.

3. See, for example, Paul A. Samuelson, "An Exact Consumption-Loan Model of Interest with or without the Social Contrivance of Money," *Journal of Political Economy* 65 (December 1958): 467-82; Henry Aaron, "The Social Insurance Paradox," *Canadian Journal of Economics and Political Science* 32 (1966): 371-74.

4. Much of this section is derived from Douglas R. Munro, "Welfare Component and Labor Supply Effects of OASDHI Retirement Benefits" (Ph.D. dissertation, Ohio State University, 1976). A more careful statement of the assumptions underlying the calculations discussed below can be found there.

5. See appendix for more detailed discussion of the assumptions underlying the calculations.

6. Munro, "Welfare Component and Labor Supply Effects," passim.

V. Sherwin Rosen: "Social Security and the Economy"

1. Paul A. Samuelson, "An Exact Consumption-Loan Model of Interest With or Without the Social Contrivance of Money," *Journal of Political Economy* 66, no. 6 (December 1958). Also, see Henry J. Aaron, "The Social Security Paradox," *Canadian Journal of Economics and Political Science* 32, no. 3 (August 1966).

2. Some analysts have gone so far as to suggest that the debt be made explicit by issuing non-transferable certificates. See James M. Buchanan, "Social Insurance in a Growing Economy: A Proposal for Radical Reform," *National Tax Journal* 21, no. 4, (December 1968).

3. See Friedman's contribution in Wilbur Cohen and Milton Friedman, *Social Security: Universal or Selective* (Washington, D.C., 1972).

4. This development shows explicitly how workers support the aged and how the projected ratio of two workers for each beneficiary around the turn of the next century, compared with the present ratio of three workers per beneficiary, will increase the burden of the system. Note that even without social security there will be relatively less workers available to support the aged.

5. Martin Feldstein, "Social Security, Induced Retirement and Aggregate Capital Accumulation," *Journal of Political Economy* 84, no. 4 (August 1976) and idem, "Toward a Reform of Social Security," *The Public Interest* (Summer 1975).

6. See Robert J. Barro, "Are Government Bonds Net Wealth?" *Journal of Political Economy* 82, no. 6 (November 1974) and Merton H. Miller and C. W. Upton, *Macro-Economy: A Neoclassical Approach* (Homewood, Ill., 1974).

7. It has been estimated that investments of this sort are of comparable magnitude with investments in physical capital. See John W. Kendrick, *The Formation and Stocks of Total Capital* (New York, 1976).

8. Alicia H. Munnell, *The Effect of Social Security on Personal Saving* (New York, 1974).

9. Feldstein, "Social Security, Induced Retirement and Aggregate Capital Accumulation," and Munnell, *The Effect of Social Security on Personal Saving.*

10. For empirical confirmation of these facts see Robert J. Barro, "Social Security and Private Savings: Evidence from U.S. Time Series" (University of Rochester, 1977).

11. Martin Feldstein, "Social Security and Private Saving: International Evidence in an Extanded Life Cycle Model," Discussion paper No. 361, Harvard University, May 1974.

12. Philip Cagan, *The Effect of Pension Plans on Aggregate Saving* (New York, 1967).

13. Alicia H. Munnell, "Private Pensions and Savings: New Evidence," *Journal of Political Economy* 84, no. 5 (September 1976).

14. Lenore Bixby, "Income of People Aged Sixty-five and Over: Overview from the 1968 Survey of the Aged." *Social Security Bulletin 33* (April 1970).

15. Colin D Campell and R.G. Campbell, "Conflicting View on the Effect of Old-Age and Survivors Insurance on Retirement," *Economic Inquiry* 14 (September 1976).

16. V. Reno, "Why Men Stop Working at or before Age 65: Findings from the Survey of New Beneficiaries," *Social Security Bulletin* 34 (June 1971).

17. William G. Bowen and T. A. Finegan, *The Economic of Labor Force Participation,* (Princeton, N.J., 1969).

18. Michael J. Boskin, "Social Security and Retirement Decisions," *Economic Inquiry* 15 (January 1977).

19. Advisory Council on Social Security, *Final Report,* (Washington D.C., 1975).

20. Friedman, *Social Security: Universal or Selective.*

21. Joseph A. Pechman, H. J. Aaron and M. K. Taussig, *Social Security: Perspectives For*

Reform (Washington D.C., 1968).

22. Henry J. Aaron, "Demographic Effects on the Equity of Social Security," paper presented at a conference of the International Economic Association, Turin, Italy, 1 April 1974.

23. Ubadigbo Okonkwo, "Individual Equity under Social Security: Some Black-White Comparisons" (University of Rochester, 1974).

VI. George Break: "Social Security as a Tax"

1. Walter W. Heller, "What's Right with Economics." *American Economic Review* (March 1975):5.

2. See, for example, John A. Brittain, *The Payroll Tax for Social Security* (Washington, D.C., 1972), chapters 2 and 3.

3. Martin S. Feldstein, "Tax Incidence in a Growing Economy with Variable Factor Supply," *Quarterly Journal of Economics* 88 (November 1974):551-73.

4. Brittain, *The Payroll Tax*, p. 59n. The lower level of tax for the self-employed was actually the result of a political compromise, but—as Brittain points out—might possibly be "rationalized on economic grounds if it were designed to exempt one-fourth of self-employed income as nontaxable imputed return to capital." Since Brittain wrote, the exempt portion has been increased to one-third.

5. Benjamin A. Okner, "The Social Security Payroll Tax: Some Alternatives for Reform," *Journal of Finance* (May 1975):577.

VII. Rita Ricardo Campbell: "The Problems of Fairness"

1. Taxes to support OASI and paid by the employee and a matching amount by the employer. This is a mechanism of payment. The burden or long-run "resting place" of the tax is generally considered to fall on the employee because otherwise these dollars would be available for wages. In cases where the demand for the product is very insensitive to price, part of the tax may be passed along to the consumer. The precise division of the burden of the tax may vary, but in the long run it is not paid by employers.

2. U.S. Congress, *Budget Options for Fiscal Year 1977,* a report to the Senate and House Committees on the Budget, 15 March 1976, p. 129.

3. It is assumed that the employee pays directly one-half of the payroll tax and although the payment mechanism is such that the employer pays the other half, the burden of the matching employer tax is primarily borne by the employee. This is because a payroll tax is part of labor costs, which the employee might alternatively receive in the form of higher wage rates.

4. The 12-quarter period is defined as 12 full quarters prior to the calendar quarter in which the covered person dies or becomes eligible for benefits.

5. Several New York City and New York State Retirement Plans paid on 1 July 1973 at age 65, and earning $14,000 in the preceding year, a net benefit (after taxes) from 99 percent to 117 percent (New York City school teachers) of the $14,000, when combined with primary social security benefits. Those with private plus social security benefit and wife's social security benefit received from 112 percent to 129 percent. Robert Tilove, *Public Employee Pension Funds* (New York, 1976), p. 279.

6. BLS *Summary, Multiple Jobholders in 1975,* Special Labor Force Report, July 1975, Table 4, p. 4.

7. The author chaired The Subcommittee on the Treatment of Men and Women under

Social Security (With respect to Sex and Marital Status) of the Quadrennial Advisory Council on Social Security, 1974-1975.

8. Secondary benefits unlike the primary benefits are not based on the covered earnings record of the recipient.

9. U.S. 95 Supreme Court 1225.

10. U.S. 94th Congress, 1st Sess., House Doc. No. 94-75, *Quadrennial Advisory Council on Social Security,* Reports; Communication from Secretary of Health, Education, and Welfare to the Committee on Ways and Means (Washington, D.C., 10 March 1975), p. 26.

11. Ibid., p. 27.

12. Ibid., p. 29.

13. Ibid., p. 30.

14. *Quadrennial Advisory Council on Social Security,* Reports, pp. 73-75.

15. Additionally, 23 percent of working women never married; 19 percent are widowed, divorced, or deserted. For more data see H. Howard, "Families and the Rise of Working Wives," *Monthly Labor Review* (May 1976), pp. 12-19.

16. BLS Press Release, 15 September 1976, Table 1, *Civilian Labor Force.*

17. Rita Ricardo Campbell, *Social Security: Promise and Reality* (Stanford, Cal., 1977), Chapter V. The reader interested in pursuing the issue of "fairness" is referred to Chapter VI on the "Treatment of Men and Women."

VIII. Carl V. Patton: "The Politics of Social Security"

1. Joseph A. Pechman, Henry Aaron, and Michael Taussig, *Social Security: Perspectives for Reform* (Washington, D.C., 1968), p. 133; see also Committee on Economic Security, *Report to the President* (Washington, D.C., 1935).

2. Committee on Economic Security, *Report to the President,* p.5.

3. Edwin E. Witte, *The Development of the Social Security Act* (Madison, Wisc., 1962), p. 748; see also Francis J. Crowley, *Historical Review of General Revenue Financing in Social Security* (Washington, D.C., 1967), p.6.

4. Witte, *Development of Social Security,* p. 6. Witte was executive director of the Committee on Economic Security. He insisted that no member of the committee realized that payments would exceed contributions for so long a period. Such an excess would go to practically all workers entering employment before 1957, at which point the 5 percent tax rate would produce sufficient revenues during an employee's working years to finance his retirement payment.

5. During late 1934 and early 1935, Dr. Francis E. Townsend proposed a monthly pension of $200 for all citizens over age 60, no matter what their income, to be paid on the condition that they retire from gainful employment and spend the money within a month. The plan, to be financed through a transaction tax, would have cost about half of the national income at that time. See Paul H. Douglas, *Social Security in the United States: An Analysis and Appraisal of the Federal Social Security Act* (New York, 1936), pp. 69-70. The move was so popular that almost 200 congressmen were absent when the bill was introduced and it was voted down without a roll call. See Frances Fox Piven and Richard A. Cloward, *Regulating the Poor: The Functions of Public Welfare* (New York, 1971), p. 101.

Another influential bill of the time was an unemployment insurance proposal introduced into Congress in both 1934 and 1935 by Representative Lundeen of Minnesota; it provided for the payment of unemployment compensation out of general funds to all unemployed persons over age 18. The bill barred no one; its benefits were to at least equal the full prevailing wage rates, and it would be administered not by the government but by bodies elected by workers' and farmers' organizations, See Douglas, *Social Security in the United States,* pp. 74-75.

6. Douglas, *Social Security in the United States,* pp. 73, 81-82; Piven and Cloward, *Regulating the Poor,* p. 101.

7. U.S. Congress, Sentate, Advisory Council on Social Security, *Final Report,* 76th Congress, 1st Session, 10 December 1938, p. 24.

8. The type of transfer has also tended to change. In the early days of the program, the transfer was almost entirely between generations (from younger to older persons). While this is still the primary transfer, changes in social security benefits have increased transfers among contemporaries; for example, from workers to widows or disabled workers.

9. U.S. Department of Health, Education, and Welfare, Social Security Administration, *Your Social Security Account Card: What It Is, What You Do with It and Why* (Washington, D.C., 1959).

10. U.S. Department of Health, Education, and Welfare, Social Security Administration, *Social Security for Young Families* (Washington, D.C., 1976), p. 3.

11. Louis Harris and Associates, Inc., *The Myth and Reality of Aging in America* (Washington, D.C., 1975), pp. 222-24. Harris reports that 81 percent of the public agreed that "government should help support older people with the taxes collected from all Americans," with a greater percentage of persons under age 65 agreeing (83 percent) compared to persons age 65 and above (76 percent). The public feels that not only should the government provide for older, retired people, but 76 percent agree that "no matter how much a person earned during his working years, he should be able to have enough money to live on comfortably when he's older and retired." In terms of social security, 97 percent of the public feels that "as the cost of living increases, social security payments to retired people should increase also."

12. John Carroll, *Social Security Financing Revisited* (Washington, D.C., 1966), pp. 27-28. See Crowley, *Historical Review,* p. 49.

13. Two recent major publications: Consultant Panel on Social Security, *Report to the Congressional Research Service* (Washington, D.C., 1976), p. 159; Quadrennial Advisory Council on Social Security, *Reports of The Advisory Council on Social Security* (Washington, D.C., 1975), pp. 9-12.

14. In addition to published materials, the following pages draw upon my interviews with a number of individuals involved with the development of social security policy, including staff members of the Social Security Administration, the House Ways and Means committee, the Senate Finance Committee, and the Carter administration transition team. Notes on these interviews are in my personal files.

15. I have avoided direct consideration of decoupling benefits (to correct for the current overadjustment for inflation). This flaw will soon be remedied, since general agreement exists in principle to do so. The question is whether wage or price indexing will be used. For details, see Consultant Panel on Social Security, *Report to the Congressional Research Service* (Washington, D.C., 1976).

16. "Social Security: What Next?" *Newsweek,* 19 January 1976, p. 37.

17. U.S. Congress, House, Committee on Ways and Means, *Decoupling the Social Security Benefit Structure. Hearings before the Subcommittee on Social Security on H.R. 14430,* 94th Congress, 2d Session, 18 June, 23, 26 July 1976, pp. 82, 91, 104, 120.

18. Ibid., p. 36.

19. During a recent hearing on increases in the tax, for example, Illinois Representative Abner Mikva challenged former HEW Secretary David Matthews and stated the time has come "to blow the whistle" on the idea that social security is an insurance program and that the

payroll tax is somehow different from other taxes. "Social Security: No Bankruptcy—but a Need for Money," *Time,* 16 February 1976, p. 54.

20. Martin Feldstein, "Toward a Reform of Social Security," *The Public Interest* 40 (Summer 1975): 81.

21. "Propping Up Social Security," *Business Week,* 19 July 1976, p. 36.

22. AFL-CIO Executive Council, "Statement on Social Security" (mimeo, Bal Harbour, Fla, 17 February 1976), p. 2.

23. "Social Security: What Next?" *Forbes,* 1 July 1976, p. 37; "Social Insecurity," ibid., p. 91.

24. William E. Simon, "How to Rescue Social Security," *Wall Street Journal,* 3 November 1976.

25. Consultant Panel, *Report to Congressional Research Service.*

26. Quadrennial Advisory Council, *Reports,* pp. 62-63.

27. "Social Insecurity," *Forbes,* 1 July 1976, p. 91.

28. "Social Security: Big Apple Bye-Bye," *Time,* 5 April 1976, p. 72.

29. Michael Ruby and Jeff B. Copeland, "Social Security: The Dropouts," *Newsweek,* 26 April 1976, p. 89.

30. Peter F. Drucker, *The Unseen Revolution: How Pension Fund Socialism Came to America* (New York, 1976), p. 170.

31. Roger LeRoy Miller, "The Cruelest Tax," *Harpers* (June 1974), p. 27.

32. General revenues are used today in the social security program, but are limited to special payments to certain uninsured persons age 72 and older, benefits attributable to military service before 1957, noncontributing wage credits to members of the armed services after 1956, noncontributory wage credits for persons of Japanese ancestry interned during World War II, hospital insurance for the noninsured, and matching funds for Part B of Medicare.

33. Quadrennial Advisory Council, *Reports,* p. 61.

34. "Social Security: What Next?" *Newsweek,* 19 January 1976, p. 37.

35. David Pauly and Tom Joyce, "Social Security: Trouble Ahead," *Newsweek,* 24 March 1975, p. 75.

36. "Social Insecurity," *Forbes,* 1 July 1976, p. 91.

37. The Burke bill, which had 150 cosponsors, would have reduced the payroll tax rate, raised the taxable wage base, and financed one-third of all social security out of general revenues. This move, however, would still levy a tax on the poor and would not touch dividends, capital gains, interest, etc. The Nelson bill, in addition to lowering the payroll tax, would have introduced personal exemptions and deductions; general revenues would be used to absorb the cost of the deductions and to pay for future increases. See Russell Goldsmith, "Feeding the Kitty: Outmoded Social Security," *New Republic* (30 August 1975), p. 5.

38. Committee on Ways and Means, *Decoupling Social Security,* p. 106.

39. The regressiveness of the social security tax might be addressed by doing as Feldstein suggests and financing social security with an actuarially fair payroll tax and using the personal income tax to redistribute income. See Feldstein, "Toward a Reform of Social Security," pp. 94-95. This would deal with some of the objections to the tax; but income from capital gains, dividends, interest, and property still would not be used to support social security.

40. For further discussion of this aspect of national health insurance, see Aaron Wildavsky, "Doing Better and Feeling Worse: the Political Pathology of Public Health" Working Paper No. 19, Graduate School of Public Policy, University of California, Berkeley (March 1975)

41. Mary Russell, "House Committee Could Be Roadblock to Carter Programs," *The Washington Post,* 28 December 1976.

IX. Michael J. Boskin: "Social Security: The Alternatives Before Us"

1. Michael J. Boskin, "Social Security and Retirement Decisions," *Economic Inquiry* (January 1977).

2. Martin S. Feldstein, "National Saving in the U.S.," Harvard Institute of Economic Research, 1976.

3. Michael J. Boskin, "Taxation, Saving and the Rate of Interest," U.S. Treasury Department, 1976; ibid., *Journal of Political Economy* (forthcoming, 1977).

4. See *Report of the Consultant Panel on Social Security* (Washington, D.C., 1976).

5. See also Martin S. Feldstein, "Social Security, Induced Retirement and Aggregate Capital Accumulation," *Journal of Political Economy* (1974).

6. *Report of the Consultant Panel on Social Security* (1976).

7. I do not mean to suggest that there are no other policy options worth considering. If such sweeping reforms are not possible, abolition of the earnings test and increased retirement ages are probably desirable and necessary, respectively.

8. John Brittain, *The Payroll Tax for Social Security* (Washington, D.C., 1972), p. 2.

9. Other remedies for a national undersaving problem are possible. For example, once out of the recession, the government could run a surplus, or we could switch from income to consumption taxation. See Michael J. Boskin, "Taxation and Capital Accumulation," *Stanford Magazine* (1976).

GLOSSARY

Adverse Incentives Incentives created by social security which lead to adverse economic behavior, such as withdrawal from the labor force or reduced private saving.

Annuity A private form of pension, purchasable in a manner similar to insurance.

Earmarked Financing Said of taxes which fund only one program, as payroll taxes fund social security.

General Revenue Financing The reverse of earmarked financing; when a program is funded out of general government funds.

Insurance or Annuity Goal The goal of providing social insurance, i.e., annuities based on past contributions.

Intergenerational Transfers Redistribution of income between one generation and another.

Noncontributory Programs Income transfer programs which the recipients do not pay into as a condition of benefit.

Noncovered Employment Employment on which social security taxes are not paid.

OASDHI Old Age, Survivors' and Disability Hospital Insurance; a program of hospital insurance, supplementary to Medicare, having its own trust fund.

OASDI Old Age, Survivors' and Disability Insurance; the basic package of Social Security, having its own trust fund.

Pay As You Go Principle The funding principle underlying any program where present benefits are paid out of present taxes.

Primary Insurance Amount (PIA) The basic benefit paid to retired beneficiaries.

Replacement Income or Ratio Social security benefits received when regular income ceases through retirement, illness, or death. Sometimes calculated as a ratio to preretirement earnings.

Retirement or Earnings Test The feature of the social security benefit formula by which beneficiaries lose a portion of their benefits as their earnings exceed a modest amount.

Transfer, Welfare, or Social Adequacy Goal The goal of providing each elderly person, regardless of past contributions, the socially adequate or minimum replacement income.

ABOUT THE AUTHORS

MICHAEL J. BOSKIN is Associate Professor of Economics, Stanford University, where he has taught since 1971. He is frequent contributor to economics journals in the fields of labor economics and public finance.

GEORGE F. BREAK is Professor of Economics, University of California, Berkeley. His publications include *Agenda for Local Tax Reform* and (with Joseph Pechman) *Federal Tax Reform: The Impossible Dream?*

RITA RICARDO CAMPBELL has been a Senior Fellow, Hoover Institution on War, Revolution, and Peace, Stanford University, since 1968. She was a member of the Advisory Council on Social Security from 1974 to 1975 and was chairman of its subcommittee on Treatment of Men and Women (with respect to Sex and Marital Status). She has also been a member of the national Citizens' Advisory Council on the Status of Women since 1969.

EDWARD COWAN is correspondent in the Washington Bureau, *The New York Times,* specializing in economics and energy. He took his masters degree in economics from Johns Hopkins University in 1960, and is author of *Oil and Water: The Torrey Canyon Disaster.*

MARTIN FELDSTEIN has been Professor of Economics, Harvard University, since 1969. He is a member of the editorial boards of *The Journal of Public Economics; Quarterly Journal of Economics; Review of Economics and Statistics;* and *Americal Economic Review;* and he is Managing Editor of *Studies in Public Economics.*

MILTON FRIEDMAN is Professor of Economics, University of Chicago, and Nobel Laureate in Economics, 1976. Since 1971 he has been a contributing editor of *Newsweek.*

DOUGLAS R. MUNRO is Assistant Professor of Economics at the University of Alabama. His dissertation was "Welfare Component and Labor Supply Effects of OASDHI Benefits."

DONALD O. PARSONS is Associate Professor of Economics, The Ohio State University. He was Harry Sherman Research Fellow, National Bureau of Economic Research, Stanford, from 1975 to 1976.

CARL V. PATTON is Director, Bureau of Urban and Regional Planning Research, University of Illinois. His recent work includes an analysis of early retirement programs in business, industry, and academia, published in *Policy Analysis* as "A Seven-Day Project: Early Faculty Retirement Alternatives."

JOSEPH A. PECHMAN is Director of the Economic Studies Program, The Brookings Institution. He has published widely in both professional and lay journals, and is the author of *Social Security: Perspectives for Reform* (with Henry J. Aaron and Michael K. Taussig).

SHERWIN ROSEN, Kenan Professor of Economics, University of Rochester, is on leave as senior research associate at the National Bureau of Economic Research, Stanford. He has published widely in economics journals and is Associate Editor of *Journal of Econometrics, Review of Economics and Statistics,* and *Econometrica.*

W. KIP VISCUSI is Assistant Professor of Economics, Northwestern University, and was Assistant Editor of *Public Policy* from 1975 to 1976. Among his publications is *Welfare of the Elderly* (with Richard Zeckhauser), forthcoming.

RICHARD J. ZECKHAUSER is Professor of Political Economy, Kennedy School of Government, Harvard University. He is also Director of Analytic Methods Seminar, Kennedy School of Government.

INDEX

SELECTED PUBLICATIONS FROM
THE INSTITUTE FOR CONTEMPORARY STUDIES
260 California Street, San Francisco, California 94111

NO TIME TO CONFUSE—A Critique of the Ford Foundation's Energy Policy Project: *A Time to Choose America's Energy Future.*
$4.95. 156 pages. Publication Date: 2/25/75. ISBN 0-917616-01-4
Library of Congress #75-10230
Contributors: Morris A. Adelman, Armen A. Alchian, George Hilton, M. Bruce Johnson, Walter J. Mead, Arnold Moore, Thomas Gale Moore, William Riker, Herman Kahn, James DeHaven.

NO LAND IS AN ISLAND: INDIVIDUAL RIGHTS AND GOVERNMENT CONTROL OF LAND USE
$5.95. 190 pages. Publication Date: 11/19/75. ISBN 0-917616-03-0
Library of Congress #75-38415
Contributors: Benjamin F. Bobo, B. Bruce-Briggs, Connie Cheney, A. Lawrence Chickering, Robert B. Ekelund, Jr., W. Philip Gramm, Donald G. Hagman, Robert B. Hawkins, Jr., M. Bruce Johnson, Jan Krasnowiecki, John McClaughry, Donald M. Pach, Bernard H. Siegan, Ann Louise Strong, Morris K. Udall.

GOVERNMENT CREDIT ALLOCATION: WHERE DO WE GO FROM HERE?
$4.95. 208 pages. Publication Date: 11/20/75. ISBN 0-917616-02-2
Library of Congress #75-32951
Contributors: Karl Brunner, George Benston, Dwight Jaffee, Omotunde Johnson, Edward Kane, Thomas Mayer, Allan H. Meltzer.

THE POLITICS OF PLANNING: A REVIEW AND CRITIQUE OF CENTRALIZED ECONOMIC PLANNING
$5.95. 352 pages. Publication Date: 3/3/76. ISBN 0-917616-05-7
Library of Congress #76-7714
Contributors: B. Bruce-Briggs, James Buchanan, A. Lawrence Chickering, Ralph Harris, Robert B. Hawkins, Jr., George Hilton, Richard Mancke, Richard Muth, Vincent Ostrom, Svetozar Pejovich, Myron Sharpe, John Sheahan, Herbert Stein, Gordon Tullock, Ernest van de Haag, Paul H. Weaver, Murray L. Weidenbaum, Hans Willgerodt, Peter P. Witonski.

THE CALIFORNIA COASTAL PLAN: A CRITIQUE
$5.95. 192 pages. Publication Date: 3/31/76. ISBN 0-917616-04-9
Library of Congress #76-7715
Contributors: Eugene Bardach, Daniel Benjamin, Thomas Borcherding, Ross Eckert, H. Edward Frech, M. Bruce Johnson, Ronald N. Lafferty, Walter Mead, Daniel Orr, Donald M. Pach, Michael Peevey.

213

NEW DIRECTIONS IN PUBLIC HEALTH CARE: AN EVALUATION OF
PROPOSALS FOR NATIONAL HEALTH INSURANCE
$5.95. 265 pages. Publication Date: 5/17/76. ISBN 0-917616-06-5
Library of Congress #76-9522
Contributors: Martin S. Feldstein, Thomas D. Hall, Leon R. Kass, Keith Leffler,
Cotton M. Lindsay, Mark V. Pauly, Charles E. Phelps, Thomas C. Schelling,
Arthur Seldon.

PUBLIC EMPLOYEE UNIONS: A STUDY OF THE CRISIS IN PUBLIC
SECTOR LABOR RELATIONS
$5.95. 295 pages. Publication Date: 6/23/76. ISBN 0-917616-08-1
Library of Congress #76-18409
Contributors: Jack D. Douglas, Raymond Horton, Theodore W. Kheel, David
Lewin, Seymour Martin Lipset, Harvey C. Mansfield, Jr., George Meany,
Robert Nisbet, Daniel Orr, A. H. Raskin, Wes Uhlman, Harry Wellington,
Charles Wheeler, Ralph Winter, Jerry Wurf.

DEFENDING AMERICA: A NEW INTERNATIONAL ROLE
AFTER DETENTE
$13.95 (hardbound only). Publication Date: April 1977 by Basic Books (New
York) ISBN 0-465-01585-9
Library of Congress #76-43479
Contributors: Robert Conquest, Theodore Draper, Gregory Grossman, Walter La-
queur, Edward M. Luttwak, Charles Burton Marshall, Paul H. Nitze, Norman
Polmar, Eugene V. Rostow, Leonard Schapiro, James R. Schlesinger, Paul
Seabury, W. Scott Thompson, Albert Wohlstetter.

PARENTS, TEACHERS, AND CHILDREN: PROSPECTS FOR CHOICE IN
AMERICAN EDUCATION
$5.95. 250 pages. Publication Date: Spring 1977. ISBN 0-917616-18-9
Contributors: James S. Coleman, John E. Coons, William H. Cornog, Dennis
Doyle, Babette Edwards, Nathan Glazer, Andrew Greeley, Kent Greenawalt,
Marvin Lazarson, William McCready, Michael Novak, John P. O'Dwyer,
Robert Singleton, Thomas Sowell, Stephen D. Sugarman, Richard E. Wagner.